BUDDHAGHOSUPPATTI

OR

THE HISTORICAL ROMANCE
OF THE RISE AND CAREER
OF

BUDDHAGHOSA

BUDDHA GHOSUPPATTI

OR

THE HISTORICAL ROMANCE
OF THE RISE AND CAREER
OF

BUDDHAGHOSA

JAMES GRAY

GYAN

Published by

Gyan Publishing House
5, Ansari Road
Daryaganj, New Delhi-110002
Phone: 011-47034999, 9811692060
E-mail: books@gyanbooks.com

Distribution Network
gyanbooks.com
India, USA, Canada, UK, Australia, France

ISBN : 978-81-212-3163-3 (PB)
First Published, London, 1892

2nd Impression 2020

Printed at: Gyan Press, Delhi.

Buddhaghosuppatti
Author: James Gray

BUDDHAGHOSUPPATTI

OR

THE HISTORICAL ROMANCE

OF

THE RISE AND CAREER

OF

BUDDHAGHOSA

EDITED BY

JAMES GRAY

PROFESSOR OF PALI, RANGOON COLLEGE
AND AUTHOR OF "THE NÎTI LITERATURE OF BURMA," ETC.

LONDON:
LUZAC & CO.
PUBLISHERS TO THE INDIA OFFICE
1892

PREFACE.

My text of the *Buddhaghosuppatti* is based upon a palm-leaf copy I obtained from the late U. Âsara's monastery at Pazundaung, and is referred to as P. On completing my transcript. I was fortunate in finding a copy in the Shwe Dagon Pagoda Library (referred to as S.D.P.). I have also made use of a MS. belonging to the Bernard Free Library (referred to as B.F.L.). The latter shows a different recension from the other two. Not only do words and constructions in it vary, but there are several (though not very material) interpolations. Strange to say, these three copies seem to be the only ones to be found in the whole of Burma. For the purpose of a critical text, I endeavoured to secure a Sinhalese manuscript, but did not succeed; and my inquiries with regard to Mahâmaṅgala and the time in which he lived have proved somewhat discouraging. The publication of this work may perhaps elicit information which does not seem readily available at present.

In editing the *Buddhaghosuppatti*, I deemed it advisable to put together as much information as possible to be found in Burmese records regarding Buddhaghosa, otherwise I may not have trenched upon a field of inquiry which has already claimed the attention of able scholars. I have added a few notes which have no pretensions to being exhaustive, but are intended to serve as hints for young students of Pali.

The translation of the Pali text appears separately.

JAMES GRAY.

RANGOON, *February* 1892.

CONTENTS.

INTRODUCTION.

TEXT.

Buddhaghose patiṭṭhante paññavanto pi ye janâ
tesaṁ paññâpabhâ natthi Râhumukheva Candimâ.

—*Buddhaghosuppatti.*

INTRODUCTION.

OUTLINES OF THE STORY OF BUDDHAGHOSA.

BUDDHAGHOSA stands out as a grand figure in the annals of Buddhism. The colossal nature of the work accomplished by him as a translator and expounder of Buddha's words, the profound scholarship brought to bear upon that work, and the almost superhuman zeal and self-denial manifested by him to execute it, evoke the highest esteem and admiration on the part of those who have made Pâli literature a study. But that very little should be known of his personal history beyond his literary labours is indeed a matter for regret. The priest Mahâmangala has given a more detailed account of him than any other author, and we have to be thankful to him for the beautiful legend by means of which we gain an insight, or, we may rather say, a kaleidoscopic glimpse, into the life of that great divine. The legend is contained in his *Buddhaghosuppatti*, which is also known as the *Mahâbuddhaghosassa Nidânavatthu.* The narrative is intensely interesting, and one is reluctant to dissociate the legendary fancies from the meagre historical facts which underlie them. It reads, in fact, like an Arthurian romance. I here give an epitome of it.

CHAPTER FIRST.

Two hundred and thirty-six years after the Nirvāṇa of Buddha the thera Mahinda established himself in Ceylon. After his death, Buddhaghosa came into prominence

Not far from the Bodhi-tree there was a village, Ghosa, named so from the circumstance of its being the rendezvous of a large number of cowherds' children. A king ruled at that time in this village. He had a spiritual adviser and secular teacher who was a Brahman, Kesî by name. This Kesî had an accomplished wife. Now, when the Buddhist scriptures were recited in Sinhalese, others did not understand them. A thera, Kesî's friend, who was possessed of supernatural powers, reflected as to who could render the scriptures in Mâgadhese if they were recited in Sinhalese. It then dawned upon him that Ghosa, a deva prince, had the necessary qualifications. Thereupon he presented himself before Sakka, king of the devas. Sakka saluted him and asked him why he had come. Having made known his object, both went to Prince Ghosa, who, on hearing the circumstances, said, "I, great king, wish to go to a higher world; existence in the world of men is most painful and vexatious. If, however, the religion of Buddha is not well understood by men, I shall go to the world of men." Having obtained this promise, the thera announced to Kesî that his wife would conceive a son in seven days, who would turn out wise and virtuous. Ghosadevaputta resolved to die, and died, and obtained conception in the womb of Kesîbrâhmaṇî. On his birth, ten months after, the dwellers in the village made a great uproar, and he was accordingly called Ghosa. He commenced his studies at the age of seven, and within seven years acquired a knowledge of the three Vedas. One day while instructing the king, Kesî came across a knotty point in the Vedas. Not knowing either the meaning or the drift of the passage, he went home in much perplexity. Young Ghosa, however, solved the difficulty and wrote down the signification of the passage. When Kesî came to find this out, he passed the following encomium: "Though young, you have shown yourself as one who is wise. He who has such a son is exalted; he is the best of men. May you be happy like an immortal.

You be my father, I shall be your son." And when he mentioned about him to the king, the latter embraced him, and said, "Be you my son, I shall be your father."

CHAPTER SECOND.

One day Kesi's friend, the thera, came, as was his habit, to obtain food. While in the middle of the house, one of his Brahman attendants took Ghosa's seat and offered it to him. He sat down on it. This made Ghosa mighty angry. When the thera ended his meal, Ghosa said, "Bald-headed sir, do you know the Vedas, or are you acquainted with any other *manta?*" The thera replied, "I know not only the Vedas, but also another *manta;*" and then rehearsed the three Vedas, after which he washed his mouth with water from his water-pot and sat down. Ghosa, becoming ashamed, asked, "I wish to know your *manta.* Repeat it." Thereupon the thera gave a sketch of the *Abhidhammapiṭaka* in relation to meritorious, unmeritorious, and indifferent actions. Ghosa was perplexed, and asked, "What is this *manta?*" On being told it was Buddha's *manta,* he desired to become a rahan; but he was repulsed by the thera, who told him that there were great obstacles in the way of unholy laymen. One day, while reflecting on the Vedas point by point, he exclaimed, "Buddha's *manta* is priceless; Buddha's *manta* pleases me. Going to Buddha's *manta,* all sufferings disappear." He then asked his parents to allow him to become a monk. His request was granted. Accordingly his head was shaven and his beard removed, and the "odour of laymanship" dissipated by the use of the perfumed powder of sandal-wood. After submitting to all necessary ceremonies, he was invested with the yellow robe. In one month's time he attained proficiency in the three *Piṭakas,* and displayed such learning that he came to be known as "Buddhaghosa," or "Ghosa the Sage."

Chapter Third.

One day Buddhaghosa reflected, "Am I or my preceptor more advanced in Buddha's words?" The thera, knowing his mind, said, "Buddhaghosa, your thoughts please me not. If you reflect, you will see that they are not becoming a priest. Beg my pardon." Buddhaghosa, being frightened, replied, "It is my fault. Pardon me." "I shall pardon you," said the thera, "if you go to Ceylon and render Buddha's scriptures into Mâgadhese." "I shall do so," replied the other, "but I must first convert my father." When his father saw him approaching, he said, "My son's countenance pleases me. Now my son will become a layman." Buddhaghosa, however, on being questioned about it, remained silent. Afterwards he built a two-roomed house, and placing in it all necessaries in the way of food and means for cooking, he shut his father up securely. When Kesî resented, saying, "I am your father. Why do you act thus?" he replied, "True, I am your son; but you are a heretic. You don't believe in Buddha's religion, therefore have I acted so." He then frightened his father with the terrors of hell and recited some beautiful stanzas in praise of Buddha's virtues. On the fourth day of his confinement Kesî believed in Buddha and was set free.

Chapter Fourth.

After a few days Buddhaghosa set out in a boat with some merchants on his journey to Ceylon. On the same day Buddhadatta set out from Ceylon for Jambudîpa. On the third day of their being at sea, their boats, through the supernatural power of the devas, came into collision and remained stationary. They entered into conversation, and on Buddhadatta finding out the object of Buddhaghosa's voyage, he said, "I possess the *Jinâlaṅkâra* as well as the *Dhâtuvaṁsa* and the *Bodhivaṁsa*, but not the

Aṭṭhakathâs and *Ṭîkâs;* but if you render Buddha's word in Mâgadhese, make a transcript also of the *Aṭṭhakathâs*, of the three *Piṭakas*, and of the *Ṭîkâs*." Encouraging Buddhaghosa thus, he made over to him the iron stylus and medicinal plum which he himself had received from Sakka, the former for writing quickly and the latter to be used as a medicament should his back ache while writing; and he further said, "Reverend Buddhaghosa, I went before you to Ceylon to compile Buddha's word. I am old, have not long to live, and shall not, therefore, be able to accomplish my purpose. You carry out the work satisfactorily." The two then parted. Buddhadatta reached Jambudîpa, and after a time, having fulfilled all priestly duties, passed away into the Tusita heaven. Buddhaghosa arrived at Ceylon, and mooring his vessel near the Dvijathâna landing-place, remained there.

Chapter Fifth.

While Buddhaghosa was at the landing-place, two women went down to fetch water. It happened, however, that while they were ascending one's water-jar hit against that of the other and broke it. A great quarrel arose and much abusive language was interchanged. Buddhaghosa, thinking he would be cited as a witness, took the precaution of putting their abuses in writing. The case came eventually before the king, and his sealed memorandum was put in evidence, he, as a priest, being debarred from attendance in court. Judgment was pronounced on the strength of his statements and one of the women punished. The king being desirous of seeing Buddhaghosa, asked the Brahmans where he resided; but they, as heretics, being unwilling to have his worth extolled, said, "He, contrary to priestly procedure, has come for the purpose of trading. It is not befitting that you should see him." The king, however, recognised his goodness, and gave expression to his own opinion in these words:

"There are indeed many priests in the island of Ceylon, but never before has one been seen like this. He goes to heaven who honours and reverences one like him, replete in virtue, quick-witted, and highly observant of duty."

CHAPTER SIXTH.

Buddhaghosa went to pay his respects to Saṅgharâjâ the archbishop of Ceylon, and sat down behind the monks, who were assembled to hear a discourse on the *Vinaya* and *Abhidhamma Piṭakas.* The archbishop came upon a knotty point in the *Abhidhammapiṭaka*, and becoming perplexed, dismissed the congregation, and went into an inner chamber to reflect upon it. During his absence, Buddhaghosa set the signification down on a board and went away to his vessel. The archbishop, who had not solved the difficulty, was surprised afterwards to see the signification entered upon the board. On making inquiries about it from the monks, he was told that the foreign priest must have written it. He then gave orders to search for him and bring him into his presence. When he was brought, the archbishop wanted him to join his congregation, but Buddhaghosa said, "I do not wish to learn. I am a resident of Jambudîpa, and have come to render the Buddhist scriptures into Mâgadhese." Saṅgharâjâ was exceedingly pleased with this assurance, but to test his qualifications for the task, he gave him a stanza as text upon which to furnish an exposition of the three *Piṭakas.* Buddhaghosa answered, "Very well," and went away. On that very day, through a lucky aspect of the stars, he composed the *Visuddhimagga* with the greatest ease, and laying it aside, went off to sleep. Sakka stealthily carried off the work. On rising and not seeing it, he again wrote it by daylight, placed it under his head and slept. Sakka came in the middle watch of night and again carried it off. Buddhaghosa, missing this too, wrote another copy in hot haste, and tying it up in a robe, went to sleep. On awakening at dawn, he saw the two copies that had been taken away at the head of his bed. Glad in heart, he took the three copies to the archbishop. On being asked how he came by three copies, he narrated the circumstances, and when the archbishop had the three read out, the difference of even a single prefix or particle could not be discovered, and he then gave permission to render the Buddhist scriptures in Mâgadhese. The author of the *Visuddhimagga* was thenceforth known in Ceylon as "Buddhaghosa," or "The Voice of Buddha."

CHAPTER SEVENTH.

After a while, Buddhaghosa asked Saṅgharâjâ for a suitable place where he could go on with his work. A seven-storied iron structure was allotted to him. There day by day he proceeded with the work of transcription. When on his begging rounds in the morning he used to pick up fallen palm-leaves and carry them away. One day a wise, virtuous, and learned man, who was a dealer in toddy, noticing what he did, scattered a lot of palm-leaves in the place where Buddhaghosa came for his food, and having done so, concealed himself. The thera picked up the leaves and took them away. The man followed him to the place where he stayed, and was quite pleased when he saw the writing work on which he was engaged. After three months, Buddhaghosa completed his task, and, on the conclusion of Lent, apprised Saṅgharâjâ of the fact. "Well done, well done!" exclaimed the latter, and added, "Even as a blind man sees not level and unlevel places, so we see not the words of Buddha. The religion of Buddha is difficult of acquirement. We discern it easily now by virtue of your translation." The writings of Mahinda were then put in a heap seven times the height of a middle-sized elephant, in a holy spot near the great shrine and set on fire. Buddhaghosa now took leave of the priests to return to India. When he was about to embark with some merchants, certain Sinhalese priests twitted him saying, "This thera no doubt only knows the *Piṭakas.* He is not acquainted with the Sanskrit writings." This was brought to Buddhaghosa's notice by his friends, and he thereupon reported the matter to Saṅgharâjâ and requested a meeting at which he would discourse from the Sanskrit. Early the following morning he ascended the pulpit, and in order to display his knowledge of Sanskrit recited two stanzas in that language. All were confounded and amazed, and stripping themselves of their clothes and jewels, placed them at the feet of the divine. These offerings formed a pile equal in height to seven middle-sized elephants. Buddhaghosa, not desiring to have any, descended from the pulpit, saluted the priests, took leave of Saṅgharâjâ, went on board with the merchants, and set out for Jambudîpa.

Chapter Eighth.

While in the middle of the sea, Buddhaghosa gave instruction to the merchants, saying, "Just as we go on the sea depending on a ship, and the ship will reach harbour depending upon us, so, depending upon the Ship of Wisdom and Goodness, we are conveyed happily to heaven." On arriving at his destination he took leave of his friends the merchants, and went to see his preceptor, who, on being apprised of his literary performance, extended to him the pardon that had been promised. He then proceeded to his parents. They paid homage to him on seeing him and entertained him with the daintiest food, and, moreover, pardoned him his previous behaviour. When he knew that the time for his departure from this world was nigh, he took leave of his preceptor, approached the Bodhi-tree, recited two stanzas in praise of it, and, on departing this life, was born in a golden mansion in the Tusita heaven, to return to this world of men on the coming of Meteyya, the next Buddha. When he died, men and gods made a funeral pile of sandal-wood for the cremation of his body. Raising aloft his remains on a golden couch, they set fire to the pile with due decorum. His relics were taken and buried in the vicinity of the Bodhi-tree and shrines erected over them.

The above is but a sketch. The story in its entirety will be found highly diverting as well as instructive. Its unity is well maintained, and it is not wanting in incidents of romantic interest. Though a legend, the author has so skilfully interwoven circumstantial details with fictitious elements as to give it an air of high plausibility; and it will not be difficult for one who seeks a moral in every tale to draw one from this. Facts of historical value cover only a limited space on the comparatively broad canvas of the narrative, and will probably add very little to what is already known of Buddhaghosa. The story, however, brings the personality of that eminent man more vividly before our minds and enforces a greater interest in him than ever; and if it does this only, it can be safely said that it was not written in vain.

Mahâmangala, it is evident, writes from the standpoint of Sinhalese prepossession and bias. I shall, therefore, set forth the history of Buddhaghosa as found in the most trustworthy Burmese records. First and foremost of them is

THE MHANNANYÂZAWIN.

This *Yâzawin* (=*Râjavaṁsa*) was compiled at Ratanâpûra (Ava) in A.D. 1830. All such learned men as could be got together were assembled in the palace under royal orders to revise the old *Yâzawins* with a view to emendation and enlargement. A good deal of research was brought to bear upon the task, and as faithful a record as possible made of social, political, and religious events in relation to the history of Burma from the earliest times. The *Mhannanyâzawin*[1] received the stamp of authority, and thereby superseded all previous histories—the *Early Yâzawin*, *Middle Yâzawin*, *Great Yâzawin*, and *New Yâzawin*. It gives a comprehensive survey of the history of Buddhism in Burma, and the *résumé* it contains of Buddhaghosa and his career is specially valuable. I give a translation of it.

The *Great Yâzawin* states that the celebrated Buddhaghosa went over from Thaton to Ceylon to bring away the *Piṭakas*, but the *New Yâzawin* declares he went from Majjhimadesa. The account is as follows:—Up to nine hundred years of the Era of Religion, the disciples of the theras Mahâdhammarakkhita, Sona, and Uttara preserved the three *Piṭakas* orally, letters not being in use in Jambudîpa. Subsequently a Brahman youth, who resided near the Bodhi-tree, attained proficiency in the Vedas and medical books, and went about in Jambudîpa discoursing upon them. One day coming to a monastery, he discoursed most eloquently. When the mahâthera Revata listened to his rich and harmonious elocution, he pronounced him to be a learned man, and, considering what comparison he should draw, asked, "Who is this braying like an ass?" The young man replied, "So you can discern the bray of asses!" On being asked questions of this character, Revata gave satisfactory answers, but on questions about the religious law, the other was nonplussed. Revata made him a rahan, saying, "I shall teach you the Vedas," and instructed him in the three *Piṭakas*. After a time he became as distinguished as Buddha and was called Buddhaghosa. Revata, knowing that Buddhaghosa wanted to make the *Tappacchâṇodaya*

[1] For the sake of contradistinction it is also known as the *Mhannanmahâyâzawindaugyî*. *Mhannan* has reference to the glass palace in which the compilation was undertaken.

and *Aṭṭhasâlinî aṭṭhakathâs*, told him, "In Jambudîpa the Pâli exists, but there are no *Aṭṭhakathâs*. Besides, the doctrinal discourses of our teachers are not intact; these exist uncorrupted in Ceylon. The Pâli as rehearsed at the Three Councils were taken over by Mahinda. After going to Ceylon and examining the glosses of Sâriputtara and other mahâtheras, listen to the Sinhalese *aṭṭhakathâs* and put them in Magâdhese." [*Sûḷavaṁsa.*]

Dhammapâla, the twenty-fifth king of Suvaṇṇabhûmi[1] (Thaton), in the dynasty of Sîharâjâ, gave great encouragement to religion. He showed the appreciation and honour in which he held Buddhaghosa by giving him four nobles as attendants, an elephant,[2] and other valuable gifts. Buddhaghosa embarked at Bassein (Puthen[3]), proceeded to Majjhimadesa, and on his arrival there had

[1] The Burmese write this *Thuvannabhummi*.

[2] It was not unusual for distinguished rahans to receive gifts of elephants, although, from religious considerations, they could not be brought to personal use. Instances are recorded of their having been set free after being received, or being given away.

[3] Called Kusimanagara in the Kalyâṇî inscriptions and ancient writings. It is on the most western mouth of the Irawadî, and was the port of embarkation to Ceylon. Direct maritime communication between that island and Burma seems to have been established in or after the tenth century. "Puthen" was Alaungpra's name for the Talaing Kuthen—a corruption and contraction of Kusima. "We owe to the grim sarcasm of Alompra numerous changes in geographical names of British Burma. The conqueror of Pegu finding Mahâgâma (once an important city north of Prome) to compare unfavourably with the other cities of that country, such as Prome and Rangoon, considered it unworthy of the name of Mahâgâma, and with prurient pleasantry suggested that henceforth it should be called Kâma (*sensual desire*). In Bassein a fierce struggle ensued between Alompra's soldiery and the Talaings. The fight centred round a *sîmâ* (Bur. *thein*), or image-house. The town had hitherto been called Kuthein (a corruption of the Pâli Kusima, the Cosmim of the Portuguese). Alompra changed the name to Puthien, 'the hot image-house.' Dagon [Tikumbha, shortened to Tikun by the Talaings and corrupted to Dagon by the Burmese.—*Ed.*] he altered to Yangun (Rangoon). By these changes a tonal similarity between the new and old appellations was preserved, but their historical and etymological connexus destroyed."—*Forchhammer.*

drawings taken of seven sites near the Bodhi-tree—the Nerañcarâ (Lilâjan) river, the Puppagôn monastery, &c. He then made up his mind to cross over to Ceylon. [*First Yâzawin*, according to Talaing history.]

The omniscient Sakka gave him a plum (*kyazuthi*) by means of which to ward off hunger and thirst, and also an iron pen to enable him to write as much as he liked. Buddhaghosa went to the harbour of Bhaṅgarî in Dakkhiṇadesa, and arrived by ship at the island of Ceylon. [*Buddhaghosuppatti* and *Sâsanavaṁsa*.]

In a cloister of the Mahâvihâra he heard the *Aṭṭhakathâs* and the discourses of the old theras expounded by Saṅghapâla the mahâthera; and having first of all composed the *Visuddhimagga*, he translated all the *aṭṭhakathâs* into Mâgadhese. [*Sûḷavaṁsa*.]

Moreover, having studied the *Mahâpaccaritaaṭṭhakathâ*, the *Mahâaṭṭhakathâ*, and the *Kurundiaṭṭhakathâ*[1] under the teacher Buddhamitta, he composed several treatises. [Buddhaghosa's *Vinayaparivâraaṭṭhakathâ*.]

On taking leave of King Mahânâma, he presented him with an elephant and other gifts, and bringing with him the three *Piṭakas*, their *Aṭṭhakathâs*, and the *Visuddhimagga*, he was on the point of going to Jambudîpa, but just then Sakka came and said, "The Majjhimadesa tract is no place for the establishment of Buddha's religion; it should be pushed on in Paccantadesa, a tract south-east of Jambudîpa, 900 leagues (*yojanas*) in circuit, including Sarekkhettarâ, Sîripaccayâ, Râmañña, &c., in order to complete 5000 years of the religious era; take it thither." This request having been made, Buddhaghosa carried the religion to Sudhammavatî (Thaton). The whole of Râmañ-

[1] The *Mahâpaccarita*, or, properly speaking, the *Mahâpaccarîaṭṭhakathâ*, is said to have been so called because it was written in Ceylon on a raft known as "Mahâpaccarî;" the *Mahâaṭṭhakathâ* was the great commentary of Mahinda, based on the renderings adopted by the First Council under Mahâkassapa; the *Kurundiaṭṭhakathâ* is said to have been so called after the Kurundavelu monastery. *Vide* "Origin of the Buddhist Arthakathâs," *J. R. A. S.*, Art. xiv., 1871.

ñadesa was in a state of great ferment and excitement at his arrival, and went forth to meet him with offerings and festivities, and escorted him as if he were the omniscient Buddha himself. On arriving at the royal city, a pavilion was erected on a beautiful site in front of the palace, and the sacred scriptures deposited therein. At this time Anomadasî was archbishop, being a disciple in the direct line of missionaries commencing from Soṇa and Uttara, who came to Suvaṇṇabhûmi after the Third Council. During his spiritual administration missionaries preached Buddhism in Burma, the Mwan (Talaing) country, Shan land, Cochin China, Arakan, Siam, and Anam.[1] Thus, then, as now, Buddha's religion flourished far and wide in Paccantadesa. [*Sâsanavaṁsa* and *Thaton Yâzawin.*]

After the Third Council, and in the year 230 A.B. (= B.C. 313),[2] Mahâmahinda arrived in Ceylon; and from the time of Devanaṁpîyatissa (the sixth king from Vijaya), who gave a great impulse to religion, up to A.B. 450, the scriptures were propagated orally, but in the reign of Vaṭṭagâmaṇî, the twenty-fourth king of the dynasty, and in the sixth year of his reign, five hundred rahandas, perceiving that the wisdom of creatures would diminish, held a Fourth Council, called the Potthakâruḷha Council, very similar to those held before, and transcribed the *Piṭakas* upon palm-leaves. In the reign of King Buddhadâsa, the sixty-third king, an abbot Dhammakathika made a Sinhalese version of the *Sutta* and *Abhidhamma Piṭakas*; and in A.B. 946 (= A.D. 403), during the rule of King Mahânâma, the sixtieth king, the mahâthera Buddhaghosa finished an edition in Mâgadhese and came to Suvaṇṇa-

[1] I have rendered "Yun" by Anam, but Forchhammer says, "The native name of the Shan and Laos states is Yôn."—*Notes on the Early Hist. and Geog. of B. Burm.*

[2] Talaing-Burmese chronology, established independently of Sinhalese reckonings, places the Nirvâṇa of Buddha at B.C. 543, or, more strictly speaking, B.C. 543-544. The Burmese now and then accept Sinhalese dates in their writings, supposing them to be correct.

bhûmi, otherwise called Thaton,[1] in the island of Jambudîpa.

In connection with the above date, the Mhannanyâzawin observes that the *Great Yâzawin* says it was in the forty-second year of the reign of the Thaton king Thinligyaung (A.D. 344–387) that Buddhaghosa went to Ceylon, but in that year, *i.e.*, A.B. 930 (= A.D. 387), Mahânâma had not commenced to reign. There is, then, a discrepancy of fourteen years.[2] It was in the fifteenth year of King Kyaungdurit, the son of Thinligyaung, that Mahânâma became king, that is, in A.B. 946 (= A.D. 403).

THÂTHANÂLAṄKÂRA.

In 1832, or two years after the completion of the *Mhannanyâzawin*, the learned Wungyi of Ava, Sîrimahânanda, compiled the *Thâthanâlaṅkâra* (*Sâsanâlaṅkâra*), a treatise on the history of Buddhism in Burma. It is considered a work of great value and of the nature of an official record. The manuscript gives fairly detailed accounts of Buddhaghosa, based on the *Buddhaghosuppatti*

[1] Thaton = Sudhammanagara. *Sudhamma* became contracted to *Thudham* = *Thudhan* = Thaton.

[2] Considering the accuracy of the Talaing chronicles, it would appear that there must be some error in Sinhalese chronology, arising probably from the desire of making Vijaya's reign synchronise with the Nirvâṇa of Buddha. For chronological purposes, I quote the following from a rare Burmese manuscript, the *Tathâgatuppattivatthu* :—"Up to 450 A.B. (B.C. 93) the *Piṭakas* were orally preserved, but in the reign of Vaṭṭagâmani, the eighteenth king of Ceylon, five hundred rahans, seeing that they could not be perpetuated so, in order to make them permanent, had them transcribed on palm-leaves. In the reign of the sixty-second king Kittisîri, and in 830 A.B. (A.D. 287), Prince Vinda with Princess Hemamâlâ, daughter of King Kurisiva, took ship from Kaliṅga to Ceylon with the eye-tooth-relic; and after the lapse of 930 years from the Nirvâṇa of Buddha (*i.e.*, after A.D. 386), Buddhaghosa arrived in Ceylon from Jambudîpa in the reign of Mahânâma, the sixty-sixth king." With regard to Buddhaghosa nothing more is stated. The *Tathâgatuppattivatthu* was written in A.D. 1775 by Dhammânanda, and seems to be based upon the *Tathâgatuppatti* of a South-Indian rahan Ñâṇagambhîra, written during or before the tenth century.

and the *Cûḷavaṁsa*. That from the former is substantially the story of my text, except that, on the authority of the *Visuddhimagga*, the compiler substitutes Saṅghapâla for Saṅgharâga as the name of the archbishop of Ceylon. The account from the *Cûḷavaṁsa* is, for the most part, similar to that given in Turnour's *Mahâvaṁsa*, and as it is fuller than that contained in the *Mhannanyâzawin*, I reproduce it here.

In the vicinity of the Bodhi-tree there was a young man who had attained proficiency in the three Vedas, and was well acquainted with Vedic controversies and opinions, and in his debates with others elicited admiration. After travelling all over Jambudîpa he made a temporary sojourn in a certain monastery. There he entered into discussions with its superior, the mahâthera Revata. In all controversial points mooted by him he received satisfactory answers, but when Revata questioned him with regard to the transcendental doctrines of Buddha, he was unable to reply. He then asked the mahâthera what *mantas* he was acquainted with; and on being told he was acquainted with Buddha's *manta*, he expressed his desire to know the system. "If you become a rahan, you will be instructed," replied Revata. On becoming one for the purpose of studying the *manta*, he completed the study of the three *Piṭakas;* and because he was profound in scholarship and became as famous as Buddha, teachers bestowed upon him the appellation "Buddhaghosa." While with Ravata, Buddhaghosa composed the *Ñâṇodaya* and *Aṭṭhasâlinî*, and when he was on the point of applying himself to the compilation of the *Parittaaṭṭhakathâ*, his preceptor told him, "The Pâli exists in Jambudîpa, but there are no *Aṭṭhakathâs*, and the doctrinal discourses of the teachers (theras) are not intact; therefore, because there exist in Ceylon the commentaries of Sâriputtarâ and other rahandas, based on the Pâli texts as settled at the Three Councils and carried thither by Mahinda, go and reduce them into Mâgadhese for the well-being of mankind." Thereupon, Buddhaghosa crossed over to Ceylon and entered the great monastery of Anurâdhapura. After hearing the thera Saṅghapâla's recital of all the Sinhalese *Aṭṭhakathâs* and *Theravâdas*, he asked permission to work up the former. The religious assembly having given him the gâthâ "*Sîle patiṭṭhâya*," &c., said, "Show your competency by means of this stanza." Then by epitomising the three *Piṭakas* and the *Aṭṭhakathâs*, he produced the *Visuddhimagga*, containing 14,000 stanzas. He produced three copies alike and showed them to the Assembly, who, delighted with his performance, handed over to him the *Piṭakas* with the *Aṭṭhakathâs*. Having made a Mâgadhese version of the latter, he returned to Jambudîpa.

With regard to Buddhaghosa's return to Jambudîpa, the compiler of the *Thâthanâlaṅkâra* observes that as neither the *Buddhaghosuppatti* nor the *Cûḷavaṁsa* mentions the exact place to which he went, it is reasonable to conjecture that Thaton (Suvaṇṇabhûmi) was his destination, especially as the *Aṭṭhakathâ* of the *Aṅguttaranikâya* mentions the existence of an oceanic highway between it and Ceylon.

Attention may be here drawn to some marked divergences in the Burmese accounts based on the *Cûlavaṁsa* and the Pâli narrative found in Turnour's *Mahâvaṁsa*.[1] For the purpose of comparison, I give the following translation of the text in the latter:—

A young Brahman in the neighbourhood of the terrace of the Bodhi-tree was accomplished in the arts and sciences

[1] The *Cullaganthavaṁsa* of Nandapañña describes the authors of the *Mahâvaṁsa* and *Cûḷavaṁsa* as unknown. According to it, they were written by different authors (*visuṁ visuṁ katâ*). The only work ascribed to Mahânâma is the *Saddhammapakâsinî*, the *aṭṭhakathâ* of *Paṭisambhidâmagga*, but Nagomahânâma is credited with the treatise *Navaṁ Mahâvaṁsaṁ*. Only one work is ascribed to Dhammakitti, and that is the *Dantadhâtupakaraṇaṁ*. The *Piṭaka Thamaing* makes Mahânâma the author of the Aṭṭhakathâ and Ṭîkâ of the *Mahâvaṁsa* and the Aṭṭhakathâ of the *Cûḷavaṁsa*. The *Sâsanadîpaka* also ascribes the Aṭṭhakathâs of these two works to Mahânâma.

and had gone through the Vedas. He was well versed in all forms of religious belief and acquainted with the various controversies. Going about in Jambudîpa, he would engage in controversies with disputants. Having come to a monastery, he used to recite a discourse full of matter and treated comprehensively. There, a mahâthera, perceiving he was a very wise man, said, "It behooves me to humiliate him," and asked, "Who is braying like an ass?" The young man retorted, "What! know you the meaning conveyed in the bray of asses?" The mahâthera said, "I know," and made a display of his own knowledge, answered each assertion, and pointed out fallacies. "Now then," said the young Brahman, "proceed to your own system." Having incited him thus, and being unable to expound to him the signification of a text from the great *Abhidhamma,* he asked, "Whose system is this?" "The system of Buddha," replied the other. On the young man saying, "Impart it to me," the mahâthera replied, "Take holy orders." Being desirous of acquiring the three *Piṭakas,* he entered the priesthood and acquired a knowledge of them, and afterwards accepted them as orthodox, saying, "This is the only road to truth." Owing to his deep Buddha-like voice, people called him "Buddhaghosa." He was like Buddha himself on the earth. Having in the monastery there composed the treatise *Ñâṇodaya,* he then wrote the section "Aṭṭhasâlinî" on the *Dhammasaṅgaṇi.*[1] Being profoundly wise, he began to compose the *Parittaṭṭhakathâ.*[2] Seeing this, the thera Revata addressed him thus—"The Pâli text alone was brought here; here the *Aṭṭhakathâs* do not exist; so also the Thera Discourses, not being intact, are not to be found; the Sinhalese *Aṭṭhakathâs* are uncorrupted. The wise Mahinda, having examined the discourses of the all-wise Buddha, admitted by the Three Councils and chanted by Sâriputta and others, translated the *Aṭṭhakathâs* in the

[1] This is one of the books of the *Abhidhammapiṭaka.*

[2] A general commentary.

language of Ceylon, and they are now extant among the Sinhalese. Go there, and, hearing them read, translate them in the idiom of the Mâgadhese; that idiom is productive of world-wide benefit." On this being spoken, Buddhaghosa, the greatly wise one, was delighted, and departing thence, came to this island in the time of this king (Mahânâma). On arriving at the great monastery (at Anurâdhapura), he proceeded to the chief cloister (Mahâpadhâna), the finest of all the apartments in the monastery, and hearing Saṅghapâla's recital of the Sinhalese *Aṭṭhakathâs* and the Thera Discourses (*Theravâdas*) in their entirety, he came to the conclusion, "This indeed is the import of the words of the Lord of Religion," and paying respect to the religious assembly, he said, "Give me all your books in order to enable me to work up the *Aṭṭhakathâs*." Wishing to test him, they gave him two stanzas and said, "Show your competence in this; on discerning it, we shall give you all the books." By means of the *Aṭṭhakathâs* together with the *Three Piṭakas*, he made a concise compendium called the *Visuddhimagga*. Then, assembling the priests who had attained to proficiency in Buddha's doctrines under the great Bodhi-tree, he began to read it. The gods, in order to publish his profound knowledge among mankind, caused the book to disappear, but he composed it a second and a third time. On the work being produced for recital the third time, they deposited the other two volumes there in the midst of the assembly. The priests then read out the three books simultaneously. In the three, neither as regards text, sense, or sequence, nor as regards the Theravâdas and the Pâli, or words and letters, was there any discrepancy. Then the priests, being singularly pleased and delighted, repeatedly exclaimed, "Undoubtedly this is Meteyya himself!" They gave him the *Tipiṭaka* books with the *Aṭṭhakathâs*, and then, while residing in the secluded Ganthâkara monastery, he translated all the Sinhalese *Aṭṭhakathâs* by means of the Mâgadhese idiom, the root of all languages. That language of all languages was conducive to the welfare of men; all the thera teachers held it as identical with the language of the Pâli. Then all that was necessary to be done being brought to a consummation, he—Buddhaghosa—proceeded to Jambudîpa to pay homage to the Bodhi-tree.[1]

VAṀSADÎPANÎ.

This manuscript was written in A.D. 1823 by Jinâlaṅkâradhaja and records the following:—

On the death of Buddhadâsa, his son, Upatissa, became king. He was favourable to Buddhism. On his death, after a rule of forty-two years, his younger brother Mahânâma ascended the throne in A.B. 915 (= A.D. 372), and in the fifteenth year of his reign (A.B. 930 = A.D. 387) Buddhaghosa arrived in Ceylon from Buddhaghosa village in Suvaṇṇabhûmi, and reduced the *Piṭakas* together with the *Aṭṭhakathâs* into Mâgadhese from Sinhalese palm-leaf manuscripts. On the completion of this work, Mahânâma had seven years yet to reign. From the time of Devânaṁpiyatissa to that of Mahânâma sixty-one kings ruled in Ceylon. After Vaṭṭagâmaṇi, during whose reign the scriptures were transcribed in Sinhalese, forty-three kings ruled from the time of Mahâcuḷaka to that of Mahânâma, in whose time Buddhaghosa copied the *Piṭakas;* and during the 485 years that they reigned, innumerable rahans and laymen composed works in connection with Buddhism.

SÂSANAVAṀSA.

In A.B. 930 (= A.D. 387) Buddhadatta crossed from Sudhammavati[2] (Thaton) to Ceylon. He remained with

[1] Turnour's translation at page 250 of his *Mahâvaṁsa* is recommended for perusal.

[2] It is said this name was given to Suvaṇṇabhûmi after the Buddhist scriptures were brought thither by Buddhaghosa. *Vide* the account from the *Thâthanâdasinasek* given further on.

Sinhalese teachers and composed the *Jinâlaṅkâra* and its *Ṭîkâ.*[1] Having a strong bias for secular (*Lokî*) writings, he returned from Ceylon without making a copy of the *Piṭakas.* In the same year, A.B. 930, the thera Buddhaghosa arrived in Ceylon, remained with the teachers of the Mahâvihâra, and composed the *Visuddhimagga* commencing with "*Sîle patiṭṭhâya naro.*" The Sinhalese teachers being pleased with him, gave him permission to write the *Piṭakas.* It is said the *Piṭaka* repository had a door of iron grating. On his reciting the *Mahânamakkâra*[2] beginning with the words "*Sugataṁ, sugataṁ, seṭṭhaṁ,*" the door opened of itself. Having transcribed the *Piṭakas* from Sinhalese into Burmese, he returned to Sudhammavati (Thaton).

"KALYÂṆI INSCRIPTIONS" NISSAYA.

The Burmese *Nissaya* of the Kalyâṇi inscriptions (A.D. 1477) of the Râmañña King Dhammacetî Râmâdhipati (A.D. 1461–1492) gives the following record, which appears in the form of a gloss only, as the inscriptions themselves make no reference to Buddhaghosa.

After eighteen kings had ruled in Ceylon, the excellent rahandas, during the reign of King Vaṭṭagâmaṇi, seeing that the religion could not be transmitted orally, and in order that it might not be confounded with other great religious creeds, had written the *Piṭakas* and the *Aṭṭhakathâs* on palm-leaves in the Sinhalese language. In the year of religion 903 (= A.D. 360), in the reign of the

[1] This is ascribed to Buddharakkhita in the *Sâsanadîpaka*, but this work does not mention the Jinâlaṅkâra as Buddhadatta's composition. My MS. of *Cullaganthavaṁsa* ascribes the *Jinâlaṅkâra* as well as its Ṭîkâ to Buddharakkhita.

[2] This poem has been edited by me along with the *Vicitravandanâ.* It is credited with being an impromptu effusion, and is cited as an example of the marvellous skill Buddhaghosa possessed in the employment of metres. There are no less than twenty different metres in the thirty-four stanzas it contains, most of them having similar quarter-verses.

ninety-ninth[1] king of Ceylon, Mahânâma, the thera Buddhaghosa went to Ceylon from Jambudîpa and made a transcription from Sinhalese to Mâgadhese.[2]

THÂTHANÂASINASEK.

(*Based on Talaing Chronicles.*)

The late Stephen M'Kertich, a clever Burmese scholar, who was long a resident of Thaton, furnished me some years ago with the following narrative from a manuscript of some value entitled *Thâthanâasinasek*, or "*The Progress of Religion:*"—

During the time of Soṇa and Uttara's mission (B.C. 307 or 308) the religion of Buddha became firmly established in Thaton, but as the law was unwritten in the language of the country, the study of the *Piṭakas* had to be transmitted orally from one set of teachers to another in succession. This unsatisfactory mode of imparting the knowledge of the newly-founded religion was continued for nearly seven centuries under seven schools of teachers until the reign of Dhammapâla, A.B. 930, when Buddhaghosa, a priest of Thaton, crossed over to Ceylon, where, having devoted himself to the study of the Sinhalese language, he copied the whole of the three portions of the *Piṭakas* with their commentaries, and brought them over

[1] It cannot be but that "ninety-ninth" is a mistake for "fifty-ninth" and "903" for "930." I have allowed the figures to stand as I found them in my manuscript, which is the only one of the *Nissayas* I have been able to consult in which the interpolation about Buddhaghosa occurs.

[2] The "Kalyâṇi inscriptions" have a very high historical value, but only so far as they refer to Dhammacetî's mission to Bhuvanekabâhu, king of Ceylon, and his efforts to reform religion in Râmaññadesa through properly ordained rahans, twenty-two of whom had to undergo re-ordination on the sacred Kalyâṇî river near Anurâdhapura. The image-house erected near Pegu (Haṁsavati) on the return of the mission was called Kalyâṇisimâ, and the stone inscriptions ordered by Dhammacetî are known as the "Kalyâṇi Inscriptions." The palm-leaf MS. has—"Imissâ pana simâya kalyâṇîgaṅgâya sajjitâyam udakukkhepasimâyam upasampannehi bhikkhûhi samatattâ kalyâṇîsimâ ti nâmam adâsi."

to his native place. From this circumstance, Thaton, which had been known as Suvaṇṇabhûmi—(the "Land of Gold")—was now called Sudhammavati (the "Land of the True Law"). The return of the ships[1] of Buddhaghosa from Ceylon with the sacred cargo on board is said to have been celebrated with great pomp and splendour. The king, attended by all the members of royalty and the nobility, and followed by a large retinue of attendants, went down to the landing, and there, having made great offerings to the holy rahan, had the sacred writings conveyed on a white elephant under a canopy formed of the red, the gold, and the white umbrellas, into the town,[2] and

[1] It was not uncommon, as native histories tell us, for two or more vessels to have sailed in company. If the "ships" were in Buddhaghosa's service, it would perhaps show that he had a large retinue of rahans and others who assisted him in the great work for which his mission to Ceylon was undertaken. It is possible, too, that, owing to the sacred nature of the "cargo," one boat may have been specially chartered for its conveyance.

[2] This was Goḷanagara, the identical place where Soṇa and Uttara, the Buddhist missionaries from India, landed. Forchhammer in his *Notes on the Early History and Geography of British Burma* says:—"About 12 miles from the present seashore and 22 miles to the north-west of Thaton rises a range of hills which is known as the Kelasa Mountains. The central and highest summit is called the Kelasa Peak, lat. 17° 2′, long. 97° 2′. The north-eastern side of the mountain is a perpendicular precipice of massive rock. The south-western declivity is thickly wooded and slopes gently towards the plain, which extends in unbroken flatness to the ocean and the Sittang river. The summit of the southern spur is crowned by the Kyaikdiyo pagoda and the central peak by the Kelasa pagoda. . . . The Kelasa pagoda as it now stands was built by Dhammaceti. . . . Descending the stairs, the path leads to an open level place, once the site of the Kelâsavihâra, which in former times enjoyed the same renown in Suvaṇṇabhûmi as the Mahâvihâra in Ceylon. The foundation of this monastery is connected with the landing of Soṇa and Uttara, and Talaing tradition reports that Buddhaghosa, after his arrival in Râmañña, retired to this cloister. . . . The region along the western base of the mountain Ayetthima to near Kinyua was formerly known (and is still frequently called) Kulâtaik. The Talaing name is Taikkulā (pronounced Taikkalā). Though the sea-shore is now about 12 miles to the west, this place was still an important seaport in the sixteenth and seventeenth centuries. It is marked on the map of Professor Lassen as Takkala, but erroneously placed a few miles north of Tavoy. Cables, ropes, and other vestiges of sea-going vessels are still frequently dug up about Taikkulā."

placed them on view in the centre of a large *mandat* or pavilion built in front of the palace for the purpose. Immense numbers of rahans of different nationalities, such as the Burmese, Talaings (Mons), Siamese, Annamese, Linchins, Thibetans, &c., flocked in from all parts of the Buddhist world and diligently applied themselves to the study of the *Piṭakas.* Under Anomadassi—the last of the above alluded seven teachers—at the head of five hundred disciples, the sacred religion of Gotama flourished in Thaton, and many of the most Brahmanical philosophers became converts to Buddhism. With the rise of Buddhism, Brahmanism and other heretical religions which had prevailed in Thaton and its neighbouring kingdoms began to decline.

BIGANDET'S ACCOUNT.

For Sir Arthur Phayre's researches and views with regard to Buddhaghosa I must refer the reader to vols. xxxiii., xxxvii., and xlii. of the *Journal of the Asiatic Society of Bengal.*[1] Bishop Bigandet's account in the *Legend of the Burmese Buddha,* as based upon MSS. which state the period of Buddhaghosa's stay in Ceylon, is as follows:—

It is probable that there occurred at Thaton what we know to have taken place in Ceylon, namely, religion was propagated first by means of oral tradition. The first one who made an attempt to possess himself of a copy of the sacred scriptures was Buddhaghosa, a *religious* of Thaton, of the Pounha (Brahman) race. That man embarked at Thaton, which was then on or near the sea. That place is in the Râmañña country, and is inhabited by a people

[1] For further bibliography on the subject *vide* Foulkes' excellent and comprehensive paper "Buddhaghosa" in the *Indian Antiquary,* vol. xix. p. 105. Excepting Phayre and Bigandet, the reader is recommended to accept the statements of writers on Burma referred to therein with some caution. See also the excellent narrative in chap. vii. of *Saddhammasaṅgaha* in the *Journal of the Pali Text Society,* 1890.

called Moun (Muns). He sailed to Ceylon, then under the reign of Mahânâma, in the year of religion 943 (= A.D. 400). He resided three years on that island, wrote the *Piṭakas* on palm-leaves with the Burmese[1] characters, those being found written in the language and characters of Ceylon. In another manuscript we read that he translated into Pâli the scriptures which were in the language of Ceylon. Buddhaghosa remained three years in Ceylon in order to complete the work he had undertaken. During his stay in that island the people were so much pleased with him that they made him many and costly presents on his leaving their country.[2]

GENERAL REMARKS.

It will be seen that the materials I have brought together are from three sources—(1) Talaing, (2) Sinhalese, (3) Burmese. Whatever accounts the Burmese possess, have been adapted from Talaing and Sinhalese chronicles, and may be safely dismissed as of insufficient value for a rigid investigation into the history of Buddhaghosa. They had no literature—in fact, no letters till the eleventh century, when Anawratha conquered Thaton and carried away the literary treasures of its monasteries to his Burman capital. The late learned Dr. Forchhammer wrote: "A critical study of Burmese literature evolves the fact that the Burmese idiom reached the stage of a translatory language at the close of the fifteenth century, and that of an independent literary tongue not much more than a

[1] Properly speaking, the Talaing characters, which were afterwards adapted by the Burmese for their literature. According to the date given here, Buddhaghosa must have been absent six years from Thaton.

[2] This account, for the most part, accords with the *Tathágata-udâna-dîpanî.* At the time Bishop Bigandet wrote, he had access to some MSS. which are difficult to find now, all affirming that Buddhaghosa was a Brahman of Thaton. The worthy Bishop, in a recent conversation with me on the subject, expressed himself as fully convinced that the famous divine went from Thaton to Ceylon (visiting Gaya first) to obtain the Buddhist scriptures for the Talaings.

century ago." As for the Sinhalese accounts, they are rendered suspicious by the incorporation of mythical ingredients. The superstructure as raised in the *Buddhaghosuppatti* rests on an unreliable foundation. With a tissue of truth and a great deal of fiction, a story is recounted which, however attractive as a legend, is untrustworthy as a historical document. The narrative in the *Cûḷavaṁsa* has an unmistakable air of plausibility about it, but as the supernatural element is not absent from it, its authenticity as a whole is open to suspicion; and in the absence of chronological data, one cannot help inferring that it is a condensed version of the *Buddhaghosuppatti* legend with such variations as the exigencies of versification may have necessitated. When, however, we examine Talaing documents, we feel as if we are moving on safe ground. The records of the Talaings date back to the fourth century B.C. The researches by Forchhammer in this direction are particularly valuable. He says: "The authenticated history of the Talaings begins with the fourth century before Christ, when Soṇa and Uttara, two Buddhist missionaries, landed at Goḷanagara, a settlement of the Gangetic Gauḍas (the Gaurs) on the shores of Suvaṇṇabhummi, which comprised the coast from the Sittaung river to the Straits. The oldest Talaing inscriptions date back to the fourth century A.D., and the lithic characters are almost identical with the Dravidian-Vengi alphabet of the same period." Their state of culture and their competence to keep up regular records of events may be gathered from the following passage:—"Talaing records contain information about Southern India which, I believe, is not found in the annals of other nations of India and Indo-China; it bespeaks an intercourse with the eastern coast of the Deccan during the supremacy of Buddhism in those parts. . . . The Talaing *pârampáras*, or histories of the succession of priests, distinctly state that Dhammapâla lived in a monastery built by order of Asoka at Bhadra(-tittha) near Kâñcipura.

He must have lived after Buddhaghosa (fifth century), for he wrote the *Visuddhimaggaṭîkâ*, a scholium on Buddhaghosa's great encyclopædia of Buddhist doctrine. . . . The list of rahans of Southern India is given in Talaing records in chronological order. . . . They give us further information for which we seek in vain elsewhere in works written in Southern India: Kaccâyana, who must have lived in about the seventh century A.D., is followed by Buddhaphira, author of *Sattasaṅgaha;* then by Ñâṇagambhira, who wrote the *Tathâgatuppatti*, a biography of Buddha. Next in order comes Anuruddha Âcariya, the author of the celebrated *Abhidhammatthasaṅgaha*. . . ." There is unmistakable evidence in Talaing records of methodical treatment and general truthfulness; and credence can therefore be easily accorded to the account they contain of Buddhaghosa. It is plainly recorded. No mythical elements go to mar its authenticity, and it is free from any great exaggeration of commonplace incidents. If he is called a native of Thaton, it is not meant that he was a Talaing. It is admitted he was a Brahman and is usually described as a rahan of Thaton. There is nothing incongruous, however, in considering it his birthplace. Thaton, or rather its Port Goḷanagara (Bur. Kulataik[1]), contained a flourishing Brahman colony, with regular maritime communication with the Deccan; and the great Kelâsa monastery, about ten or twelve miles south-east of the port, was the home of a large number of Buddhist rahans of the Brahmanic race.

The main facts, therefore, in the history of Buddhaghosa, based upon Talaing history and tradition, will be as follows:—Buddhaghosa was a Brahman born in Thaton. He was an inmate of the Kelâsa monastery, and in A.D.

[1] "Kulataik" signifies "a brick or mud building of the Kalas (or Golas = gauḍas)." As to the origin of the name Goḷanagara, the MS. of the Kalyâṇi inscriptions has—"Taṁ pana nagaraṁ Goḷamanussagharânaṁ viya mattikagharânaṁ bahulatâya Goḷamattikanagaran ti yâv' ajjatanâ voharanti."

387 he was deputed to Ceylon by King Thin-li-gyaung (Dhammapâla) in order to bring away a copy of the Buddhist Scriptures. At Bassein he took ship for Tâmalitti, the Indian port, and first went to Gayâ by the Gangetic route, to obtain drawings of the principal sacred sites. He returned by the same route and proceeded to Ceylon. He stayed there three years. He composed the *Visuddhimagga* while at Anurâdhapura, and on his return to Thaton brought a complete copy of the *Piṭakas* with their commentaries, as well as other works[1] in the Talaing (Dravidian-Vengi) characters.

With regard to the means of communication, recent archæological researches show that there was a regular sea-route between Gauḍa and Kalinga and the port of Goḷanagara, about thirty miles north-west of the present town of Thaton. Up to the tenth century there was no direct communication between Suvaṇṇabhûmi and Ceylon but *viâ* some port[2] on the eastern Indian coast. This fact would explain the reference to Buddhaghosa going to India[3] before proceeding to Suvaṇṇabhûmi, and when on

[1] It is now known on good authority that he brought with him several Hindoo law-books, which were adapted by native jurists for Talaing requirements. The Burmese law treatises were subsequently based on these.

[2] The principal ports appear to have been Nâvutapaṭṭana and Komâlapaṭṭana. There was also the port of Nâgapaṭṭana, an entrepot of trade with Ceylon. The two former had a regular service of vessels to Bassein in Râmaññadesa, which subsequently became absorbed in Marammadesa (Burma). Buddhaghosa, in order to get to the nearest Indian port on his journey to Buddhagayâ (then called only Gayâ), may have proceeded from Goḷanagara *en route* to Bassein (Kusimâ), but first going to Haṁsavati (Pegu). A MS. history of the reign of King Dhammacetî records the voyage of a vessel which started at Bassein and went coasting, touching at the principal ports of Arakan and Eastern Bengal. It had on board the members of the mission sent by that king to Gayâ in A.D. 1472. The Kalyâṇî inscriptions give the account of two ships that went direct to Ceylon from Bassein.

[3] India is often called Jambudîpa, although the latter name properly includes Further India as a division (Paccantadesa, with the districts of Sunaparanta, Sirikhettara, Ramañña, Suvaṇṇabhûmi, &c.). In relation to Ceylon Jambudîpa implies the great southern continent.

his way to Ceylon from Buddha Gayâ he may have met Buddhadatta in some monastery in Kalinga or elsewhere on the coast.

There may be some significance in the statement that Buddhaghosa compiled three editions of the *Visuddhimagga*. The original compilation was most probably intended for Thaton, while one copy may have been made for India, and the other for retention in the Mahâvihâra of Anurâdhapura. As to the duration of Buddhaghosa's stay in Ceylon, the *Buddhaghosuppatti* says it was three months. This calculation is, no doubt, the outcome of Mahâmaṅgala's ingenuity to make the divine's performances accord with the miraculous capabilities of the celestial style presented to him by Buddhadatta. Three years, as mentioned in Talaing chronicles, also seem insignificantly small for the colossal work attributed to him. It is reasonable, however, to suppose that he had able coadjutors, and was assisted by scribes, who may have written to his dictation, or served as ordinary copyists. The first *Yâzawin* says he brought away in all fifty-six volumes.[1] If it be admitted that the Sinhalese of the fourth century A.D. was only a dialectical variety of the Mâgadhese proper—and I believe this cannot be controverted—it must have been a work chiefly of adaptation rather than of translation that Buddhaghosa had to perform. The *Aṭṭhakathâs*, no doubt, received his special attention, while the transliteration of the *Piṭakas* may have been executed in collaboration. Therefore, taking into consideration his genius and attainments, a period of three years as the duration of his stay in Ceylon is not below the mark.

It seems unreasonable to hold that a special deputation from the mahâthera of Gayâ, under the circumstances recorded by the Sinhalese writers, was required for the pur-

[1] Six centuries afterwards, when Anawratha conquered Thaton, it is said in the history of Pagan that the Burmese carried away to their capital five elephant-loads of manuscripts.

pose of obtaining the commentaries.[1] Buddhism was in a flourishing condition in Behar and the southern countries at the end of the third and the beginning of the fourth century, as attested by the Chinese pilgrim Fa Hian, and no disastrous or paralysing effect on its ascendency is recorded in the centuries preceding. Buddhist monasteries abounded at the time of that pilgrim's visit. Able rahans must have existed in large numbers, and writing was not unknown. It seems difficult, therefore, to accept the statement that the commentaries were lost completely in India, or that, with easy communication between it and Ceylon, the desideratum could not have been readily supplied without having recourse to an improbable story.[2] In Thaton, however, where the labourers in the missionary field were comparatively few, and where up to the fourth century the scriptures were preserved orally, the necessity for the possession of a complete version with commentaries must have been keenly felt. That the king of Thaton, by the advice of the chief of the Kelâsa monastery,

[1] When Fa Hian visited Gayâ, he found three monasteries there which conformed to the orthodox Buddhist regulations. He says nothing about any Sinhalese priests or monastery. But see Oldenberg's *Vinaya Piṭaka*, p. liii.

[2] During the three years Fa Hian was at Sâvatthî he collected several sacred books, and for two years previous to his leaving for Ceylon he was engaged in copying the scriptures at Tâmalitti, a flourishing Buddhist town. He had difficulties at first in obtaining certain works, but these must have disappeared to a great extent after he had devoted himself to the study of Sanskrit and was able to converse more freely and intelligently with the Buddhist rahans than on his arrival in India. The bulk of the books he acquired was from the Gangetic monasteries. He does not tell us about the state of literature in Ceylon, but, says Beal, "continuing his search (for the sacred books), he obtained a copy of the *Vinaya Piṭaka* according to the school of the Mahisasikas." He also obtained three Sinhalese compilations in Pâli. He says nothing about the *Aṭṭhakathâs*, but these, as being in Sinhalese, he could not have readily utilised. And here a very pertinent question may be asked. If Buddhaghosa took the commentaries to Gayâ, to Revata's monastery, how is it Fa Hian, who was in eager search for manuscripts, makes no mention of them? The theory that Buddhaghosa was sent from Gayâ on his literary mission to Ceylon is open to grave suspicion, and may be safely interpreted as a mere fabrication.

should have sent a religious mission under Buddhaghosa is a most likely inference, and taken in connection with the unvarnished statements of the Talaing chroniclers, enforces implicit credence.

BUDDHAGHOSA'S WORKS.

As no account of Buddhaghosa would be complete without mention of his literary works, I give two lists from Burmese MSS. The nomenclature differs, but the treatises included are identical. The Burmese *Piṭakathamaing* names the following *Aṭṭhakathâs* by him :—

Pârâjikaa°.	Ekanipâtaaṅguttaraa°.
Pâcityâdia°.	Dukatikacatukkanipâtaa°.
Saṅkhâvitaraṇîa°.	Pañcâdinipâtaaṅguttaraa°.
Suttasîlakkhandhaa°.	Khuddakapâṭhaa°.
Suttapâtheyyaa°.	Dhammapadaa°.
Suttamahâvâa°.	Suttanipâtaa°.
Mûlapaṇṇâsaa°.	Apâ lânaa°.
Majjhimapaṇṇâsaa°.	Visudhimaggaa°.
Uparipaṇṇâsaa°.	Aṭṭhasâlinîa°.
Sagâthâvârasaṁyuttaa°.	Sammohavinodanîa°.
Saḷâyatanamahâvârasaṁyuttaa°.	Pañcapakaraṇaa°.

Nidânakhandhavârasaṁyuttaa°.

The *Culiaganthavaṁsa* of Nandapaññâ gives the following list :—

(1.) Visuddhimagga.
(2.) Sumaṅgalavilâsinî, commentary of Dîghanikâya.
(3.) Papañcasûdanî, „ Majjhimanikâya.
(4.) Pakâsinî „ Saṁyuttanikâya.
(5) Manorathapuṇî, „ Aṅguttaranikâya.
(6.) Samantapâsâdikâ, „ Pañcavinayagantha.
(7.) Paramatthakathâ, „ Sattâbhidhammagantha.
(8.) Kaṅkhavitaraṇîvisuddhi, „ Pâtimokkha.
(9.) Khuddakapâṭhaa°. (10.) Dhammapadaa°. (11.) Jâtakaa°.
(12.) Suttanipâtaa°. (13). Apâdânaa°.[1]

---

[1] The existing *Aṭṭhakathâs* are thus enumerated by Childers :—
(1) *Samantapâsâdikâ* [commentary on the Vinaya]; (2) *Kaṅkhâvitaraṇî*

The first great work of Buddhaghosa, the *Visuddhimagga*,[1] has been appropriately termed a "marvellous production," and if he had written nothing else, it alone would have secured him undying fame. But when we scrutinise his numerous commentaries and become conscious of the genius they display, we are almost staggered with the immensity of his work. He, says Professor Childers, was "one of the most extraordinary men that Buddhism has produced. Buddhaghosa did not confine himself to translating Mahendra, but incorporated other old Sinhalese chronicles existing in his time, and added immense contributions, chiefly exegetical, of his own. Much of the matter his commentaries contain is as old as the Tripiṭaka itself, while, like the Tripiṭaka, they are rich in history and folklore, and abound in narratives which shed a flood of light on the social and moral condition of ancient India." No doubt, he has left a rich legacy of literature to Burma, Siam, and Ceylon. Suvaṇṇabhûmi in particular has good reason to be proud of him. Siam derived the Buddhist scriptures from her, as is clear from Talaing chronicles, and the debt of gratitude which Burma owed to Ceylon was sufficiently repaid when, after the total destruction of Sinhalese Buddhistic literature by the Malabars in the twelfth century, she was able to return to that sacred island a copy of the very books she had borrowed seven cen-

[c. on Patimokkha]; (3) *Sumaṅgalavilâsinî* [c. on Dîghanikâya]; (4) *Papañcasûdanî* [c. on Majjhimanikâya]; (5) *Sâratthappakâsinî* [c. on Saṁyuttanikâya]; (6) *Manorathapûraṇî* [c. on Aṅguttaranikâya]; (7) *Paramatthajotikâ* [c. on Khuddakanikâya and Suttanipâta]; (8) *Dhammapadaṭṭhakathâ*; (9) *Paramatthadîpanî* [c. on Udâna, Vimânavatthu, Petavatthu, and Theragâthâ]; (10) *Abhidhammatthadîpanî* [c. on Ittivuttaka]; (11) *Jâtakaṭṭhakathâ*; (12) *Saddhammapajjotikâ* [c. on Niddesa]; (13) *Saddhammappakâsinî* [c. on Paṭisambhidâ]; (14) *Visuddhajanavilâsinî* [c. on Apâdâna]; (15) *Maduratthavilâsinî* [c. on Buddhavaṁsa]; (16) *Cariyâpiṭakaṭṭhakathâ*; (17) *Atthasâlinî* [c. on Dhammasaṅgani]; (18) *Sammohavinodanî* [c. on Vibhaṅga]; (19) *Pañcappakaraṇaṭṭhakathâ* [c. on the Five Pakaraṇas].

[1] No Talaing record makes mention of any work of Buddhaghosa prior to the *Visuddhimagga*.

turies before and preserved with the most jealous care.[1] Buddhaghosa, it seems to me, was but a thera of profound knowledge in the estimation of the Sinhalese until their scriptures were restored to them. Then only was he magnified into a legendary personage and made the hero of a mythical romance.

THE AGE OF THE *BUDDHAGHOSUPPATTI.*

I have not been able to obtain anything but the vaguest information in Burma with regard to Mahâmaṅgala and the age of the *Buddhaghosuppatti.* I have, however, to express my indebtedness to the Director of Public Instruction, Colombo, for the following communication :—"There is no record of a Sinhalese author by the name of Mahâmaṅgala, but there was a man by the name of Maṅgala and two men by the name of Sumaṅgala. Maṅgala was not the author of any existing works, but was the tutor of Vedeha, the author of Sidatsaṅgarava, Rasavâhinî, and Samantakûṭavaṇṇanâ. He lived in the thirteenth century." It is out of the question to identify the author of *Buddhaghosuppatti* with one of the Sumaṅgalas, especially with the writer of the two well-known Ṭikâs, but in the absence of more precise information, I am disposed to identify him with Maṅgala, the tutor of Vedeha. The

[1] Buddhaghosa's commentaries as they now exist in Ceylon were taken over from Pagan in Burma. No copy of them could have been kept by the Sinhalese priests after he first compiled them, otherwise Fa Hian, who visited Anurâdhapura after Buddhaghosa, would most certainly have mentioned them, and taken at least a copy of the commentary on the Vinaya. Mahinda's commentaries, which were of little use to the Chinese pilgrim, must have existed then. The exact manner of the disappearance of Mahinda's writings has never yet been satisfactorily explained. If Mahâmaṅgala, who says he writes "yathâbhûtaṁ" ("according to reality"), is to be credited, they were consigned to the flames when Buddhaghosa had compiled his own commentaries ; but the allusion in the *Buddhaghosuppatti* (chap. vii.) to the burning of the manuscripts seems to me allegorical of their destruction by the Malabar conquerors of Ceylon. It is possible, however, that Mahâmaṅgala refers only to the particular copy that Buddhaghosa had made use of.

internal evidence of the text, as resting chiefly on the allusion to the burning of Mahinda's manuscripts, and interpreted by me as referring to the destruction of them by the Malabars, points approximately to the thirteenth century as the period when the Piṭakas and their commentaries were taken to Ceylon from Burma, and Buddhaghosa looked upon as some extraordinary person by the Sinhalese, and made the hero of a legendary narrative.

That the text is comparatively old is evidenced by the ridiculously corrupt form in which the Sanskrit stanzas (chap. vii.) have come down. It is well known that Sanskrit in Burma, during the last three centuries, or perhaps even more, has been appropriately transliterated by means of the usual Burmese characters, with the addition of a few conventional symbols. This conventional system was evidently unknown when the *Buddhagosuppatti* was transcribed for Burmese use. But the difficulty still is, How happens it that Mahâmaṅgala and his work are not known in Ceylon? Did the thera write the work in Pagan, intending it to be taken to Ceylon, but not live to do so? That he was a Sinhalese is indicated in a gloss which renders "imasmiṁ patiṭṭhahati" at the commencement of chapter i. of the text by "imasmiṁ Laṅkâdîpe patiṭṭhahati." The question also suggests itself, Could this Maṅgala or Mahâmaṅgala have been associated with the conveyance of the Buddhist scriptures and their commentaries from Burma to Ceylon?

BUDDHAGHOSUPPATTI.

BUDDHAGHOSUPPATTI.

Namo tassa bhagavato arahato sammâsambuddhassa.

INTRODUCTION.

Vanditvâ ratanattayaṁ sabbapâpapavâhanaṁ
Buddhaghosassa uppattiṁ vaṇṇayissaṁ[1] yathâbhûtaṁ:
bhavantâ sâdhavo tumhe sappurisâ samâgatâ
aññañca kammaṁ pahâya taṁ[2] suṇâtha samâhitâ;
yo ca sutvâna saddhammaṁ vâceti[3] api sikkhati
diṭṭhe dhammo ca pâsaṁso pacchâ nibbânapâpuṇi;
tasmâ suṇeyya sakkaccaṁ Sammâsambuddhavaṇṇitaṁ
Buddhaghosassa nidânaṁ saggamokkhasukhâvahan ti.

CHAPTER FIRST.

BOYHOOD.

EVAṀ iddhiyâdîhi saddhiṁ âgantvâ paṭhamaṁ tâva[4] âyasmâ Mahindathero sammâsambuddhassa parinibbânato dvinnaṁ vassasatânañca upari chattiṁ same vasse ca imasmiṁ[5] patiṭṭhati. Patiṭṭhahitvâ ca[6] yâvatâyukaṁ tiṭṭhamâno bahûnaṁ vâcetvâ bahûnaṁ hadaye patiṭṭhapetvâ anupâdisesâya nibbânadhâtuyâ parinibbâyi. Tassa aparabhâge Buddhaghoso nâma thero uppajji. Tassa ca uppannabhâvo kathaṁ veditabbo. Ekasmiṁ kira samaye Ghoso nâma gâmo mahâbodhito avidûre ahosi. Kasmâ bahûnaṁ gopâladârakânaṁ bâhullanivâsanaṭhânabhûtattâ[7] gâmassa Ghosagâmo nâma ahosi. Tasmiṁ aññataro[a] râjâ·

[1] P.S.P. vaṇṇayissâmi. [2] S.D.P. daṁ = idaṁ. [3] S.D.P. vâcati, P. vâcâhi. [4] Paṭhamaṁ tâva is the reading of the B.F.L. MS.; other MSS. have patiṭṭhanto ca. [5] Imasmiṁ = imasmiṁ Sîhaḷadîpe. [6] Pana. [7] B.F.L. bâhullasannipâtaṭhânabhutattâ.

rajjaṁ kâreṣi. Tassa Kesî nâma brâhmaṇo purahito seṭṭhagaru pi ahosi pîyo manâpo. Tasseva bhariyâ Kesiṇî nâma ahosi. Tenâhu porâṇâ—

> Kesî ca nâma brâhmaṇo rañño ca vallabho piyo
> vedattayaṁ sikkhâpeti râjânañca dine dine;
> tasseva Kesiṇî nâma brâhmaṇî ca visâradî
> Brâhmaṇassa pîyâ hoti garuṭṭhâ va[1] anâlasâ ti.

Yadâ pana pariyattisâsanasseva Sîhaḷabhâsâya kathitattâ aññe pariyattisâsanaṁ na vijânanti, tadâ aññataro thero iddhipatto mahâkhîṇâsavo taṁ kâraṇaṁ jânitvâ cintesi—"Ko nâma mahâthero Bhagavato pariyattiṣâsanaṁ Sîhaḷabhâsâya parivattetvâ Mâgadhabhâsâya kathessatî" ti. Cintetvâ ca pana Ghosadevaputtaṁ Tâvatiṁsabhavane vasantaṁ Bhagavato pariyattisâsanaṁ Sîhaḷabhâsâya parivattetvâ Mâgadhabhâsâya kathetuṁ samatthan ti addasa.[2] Cintanantaram eva Tâvatiṁsabhavane Sakkassa devarañño pâturahosi.

Sakko pi taṁ theraṁ vanditvâ pucchi—"Kiṁkâraṇâ bhante âgatosî" ti. So pi "Dâni Mahârâjâ Bhagavato sâsanaṁ aññehi dubbijânaṁ[3] hoti Sîhaḷabhâsâya kathitattâ; Ghosadevaputto nâma pana eko devo Tâvatiṁsabhavane santo so pi [b]tihetukapaṭisandhipañño[4] pubbabuddhesu katasambhâro samattho Bhagavato sâsanaṁ Sîhaḷabhâsâya parivattetvâ Mâgadhabhâsâya[5] kathetun" ti âha.

Sakko pi "Tena hi bhante âgamehî" ti vatvâ Ghosadevaputtassa santikaṁ gantvâ âliṅgetvâ âha "Mârisa devaputta eko mahâthero tvaṁ[6] ârâdhetvâ manussalokaṁ gamituṁ icchatî" ti.

So "Devarâja ahaṁ uparidevalokaṁ gamituṁ icchâmi; kasmâ manussaloke nivâso nâma bahudukkho bahupâyâso; tena manussalokaṁ na gacchâmi; yadi pana

1 B.F.L. visuddhatâ for garuṭṭhâ va. 2 Three MSS. have adassa. 3 B.F.L, S.D.P. duvijânaṁ. 4 B.F.L. tihetukapaṭisandhi nâma sappañño. 5 B.F.L. adds mûlabhâsâya. 6 S.D.P. tuvaṁ, B.F.L. taṁ.

Bhagavato sâsanaṁ aññehi dubbijânaṁ[1] hoti ahaṁ pi manussalokaṁ gamissâmî" ti anujâni.

Sakko devarâjâ tassa paṭiññaṁ gahetvâ therassa paṭivedesi. So thero devaputtassa paṭiññaṁ laddhâ puna âgacchi.

Tadâ so thero Kesîbrâhmaṇasahâyo kulupako ahosi. Vibhâtâya rattiyâ pattacîvaraṁ âdâya gantvâ Brâhmaṇassa gehe paribhuñji. Bhuttâvasâne brâhmaṇaṁ âha—"Ajjadivasato[2] paṭṭhâya sattame divase mâ pamajja; tava putto bhavissati mahâpuñño mahâpañño" ti vatvâ ca pana pakkami.

Sattame divase Ghosadevaputto adhiṭṭhahitvâ kâlaṁ katvâ Kesiṇiyâ brâhmaṇiyâ kucchimhi paṭisandhiṁ gaṇhi. Dasamâsaccayena gabbhato nikkhami. Nikkhamanakâle ca dâsakammakarâdayo brâhmaṇaparisâ aññamaññaṁ sundaraghosasaddâni "khâdatha pivathâ" tiâdini pavattayiṁsu. Tenassa Ghosakumâro ti nâmaṁ akaṁsu.

So pi sattavassiko hutvâ vedâni ca uggahetvâ sattavassabbhantare yeva tiṇṇaṁ vedânaṁ [d]nipphattiṁ pâpuṇi. Ekasmiṁ divase Ghosabrâhmaṇakumâro Bissanukhandhe nisîditvâ mâsaṁ bhuñjati.[3] Atha naṁ Ghosakumâraṁ Bissanukhandhe nisîditvâ mâsaṁ bhuñjantaṁ disvâ aññe brâhmaṇâ atikuddhâ "Hare[4] Ghosakumâra kasmâ tvaṁ amhâkaṁ [e]âcariya Bissanukhandhe[5] nisîditvâ [f]mâsaṁ bhuñjasî" ti. "Api ca attano garubhâvamattaṁ na jânâti kathaṁ tvaṁ tayo vede jânissasî"[6] ti âhaṁsu. So Bissanukhandhe nisîditvâ mâsaṁ bhuñjanto yeva Bissanukiccaṁ pucchanto gâthamâha—

> **Mâso va bissanu nâma ko [g]bissanû ti vuccati**
> **ubhayesu ca etesu kathaṁ jânâmi bissanû ti.**

Taṁ sutvâ brâhmaṇâ aññamaññaṁ mukhaṁ olokayamânâ paṭivacanaṁ dâtuṁ asamattho [h]apaṭibhâṇâ va ahesuṁ. Athaññe[7] brâhmaṇâ taṁ Kesîbrâhmaṇaṁ ârocesuṁ.

[1] B.F.L. dujânaṁ. [2] S.D.P. ajjato. [3] S.D.P bhuñji. [4] S.D.P. are.
[5] B.F.L. âcariyo hutvâ Bisanukhandhe. [6] S.D.P. and P. na jânâsi.
[7] S.D.P. atha.

Kesîbrâhmaṇo attano puttaṁ pucchi—"Kiṁ tâta evaṁ karosî" ti.

"Âma tâtâ" ti.

Kesîbrâhmaṇo brâhmaṇe 'palobhetvâ "Maṁ passatha, mâ kujjhi; so taruṇo, kiñci na jânâsî" ti uyyojesi.

Ekasmiṁ divase Kesîbrâhmaṇo râjânaṁ vedaṁ sikkhâpetuṁ attano puttaṁ gahetvâ sikkhanatthâya gato hoti. Ghosabrâhmaṇakumâro gamituṁ ajacammaṁ âsanaṁ gahetvâ pitarâ saddhiṁ gato hoti. So râjânaṁ sikkhanto yeva ekasmiṁ vedapadese gaṇṭhiṭhânaṁ patvâ atthaṁ vâ adhippâyaṁ vâ ajânitvâ kaṅkho hutvâ râjânaṁ âpucchitvâ aṭṭagehaṁ punâgacchi.

Ghoso attano pitaraṁ gaṇṭhiṭhânaṁ ajânantaṁ ñatvâ attano paññâya taṁ gaṇṭhiṭhânaṁ 'uttânaṁ katvâ potthake likhitvâ ṭhapesi. So pi Kesibrâhmaṇo taṁ akkharaṁ disvâ va vedânaṁ atthañca adhippâyañca ñatvâ tuṭṭho hoti. Tassa brâhmaṇassa taṁ gaṇṭhiṭhânaṁ manasi pâkaṭaṁ hoti. Atha so Kesîbrâhmaṇo parijane[1] pucchi—"Idaṁ akkharaṁ nâma kena likhitan" ti.

Parijanâ âhaṁsu—"Tâta taṁ akkharaṁ nâma kena[2] tava puttena likhitan" ti.

Kesîbrâhmaṇo attano puttaṁ pucchi—"Tâta taṁ akkharaṁ nâma tayâ likhitan" ti.

"Âma tâtâ" ti vadati.

So ativiya tuṭṭho attano puttaṁ pasaṁsanto dve gâthâyo abhâsi—

> Tvaṁ yeva daharo hoti paññavâ ti ca pâkaṭo
> yassa tvaṁ tâdiso putto so seṭṭho va januttamo.
>
> Tvañca dâni sukhî hosi amaro viya saṇṭhito[3]
> tvaṁ yeva me pitâ hosi, ahaṁ te puttasannibho ti.

Evaṁ pi so attano puttaṁ pasaṁsitvâ râjânaṁ ârocesi. Râjâ taṁ sutvâ ativiya tuṭṭho taṁ âliṅgetvâ aṅke[4] katvâ

[1] S.D.P. parijanaṁ. [2] B.F.L. P. tena. [3] B.F.L. attato. [4] S.D.P. aṅge. B.F.L. omits aṅke katvâ.

sîsaṁ cumbitvâ âha—"Tâta tvaṁ mama putto hosi; ahaṁ te pitâ" ti vatvâ imaṁ gâtham âha—

Varapañño tuvaṁ tâta brâhmaṇesu ca uttamo;
paññâya te pamodâmi; dammi te varagâmakan ti.

iti Buddhaghosakumârabhûtassa
paṭhamaparicchedavaṇṇanâ
samattâ.

CHAPTER SECOND.

ADMISSION TO THE PRIESTHOOD.

TATO paṭṭhâya brâhmaṇa-Ghosakumârassa vedaṁ uggaṇhantassa divase divase ca chasahassavedapadâni[1][a] vâcuggatâni honti. Athekadivase Kesîbrâhmaṇasahâyo mahâthero attano pakatiyâ bhojanatthâya gehaṁ gantvâ gehamajjhe tiṭṭhati. Atheko mâṇavo Ghosabrâhmaṇakumârassa âsanaṁ âharitvâ paññâpetvâ mahâtherassa adâsi. Mahâthero upekkhako va hutvâ Ghosabrâhmaṇakumârassa âsane nisîdi. Atha kho Ghosabrâhmaṇakumâro taṁ mahâtheraṁ attano âsanne nisinnaṁ disvâ ativiya kodho hutvâ pahaṭanaṅguṭṭhabhujago[2] viya ahosi. So taṁ kujjhitvâ avisahanto mahâtheraṁ akkosi—"Ayaṁ muṇḍasamaṇo alajjî attano pamâṇaṁ na jânâti; kasmâ me pitâ bhojanaṁ dâpesi; kinnu ayaṁ imaṁ vedaṁ jânâti udâhu aññaṁ mantaṁ jânâtî" ti. Paribhâsitvâ ca pana evaṁ cintesi—"Ahaṁ bhuttâviṁ oṇitapattapâṇiṁ[3] muṇḍasamaṇaṁ imaṁ vedaṁ pucchissâmî" ti.

Atha so mahâtheraṁ bhuttâvioṇitapattapâṇiṁ nisinnaṁ pucchi—"Bhante muṇḍa tvaṁ vedaṁ jânâsi udâhu[4] aññaṁ mantan" ti.

Mahâthero taṁ sutvâ ativiya haṭatuṭṭho[5] hutvâ âha—"Tâta Ghosa ahaṁ tumhâkaṁ vedaṁ jânâmi, aññaṁ mantaṁ pi jânâmî" ti.

So âha—"Yadi vedaṁ jânâsi tvaṁ sajjhâyaṁ karohî" ti.

Atha mahâthero tayo vede sajjhâyitvâ tiṇṇaṁ vedânaṁ âdimajjhantaṁ [b]âmasitvâ[6] paṇḍitena vinivedaṁ jaṭasut-

[1] P. saṭṭhi for cha. [2] B.F.L. -bhujagindo. [3] S.D.P. has nihata = nihata for oṇita. [4] S.D.P. adds kiṁ. [5] S.D.P. and P. omit haṭa. [6] S.D.P. âmassitvâ.

taṁ guḷamiva vedaṁ susaṇṭhapetvâ sajjhâyi. Sajjhâyanâvasâne attano kamaṇḍalunâ[1] udakena[2] mukhaṁ vikhâletvâ va nisídi.

So taṁ disvâ lajjî hutvâ punâha—"Bhante muṇḍa ahaṁ tava mantaṁ jânituṁ icchâmi; tava mantaṁ sajjhâhî" ti.

Mahâthero taṁ pasâdento Abhidhammamâtikaṁ sajjhâyi kusalâ dhammâ akusalâ dhammâ abyâkatâ dhammâ ti. Âdito va tiṇṇaṁ mâtikânaṁ atthaṁ vibhajanto[3] âha—"Tâta Ghosa kusalaṁ nâma anavajjiṭṭhavipâkalakkhaṇaṁ akusalaviddhaṁsanarasaṁ vodânapaccupaṭṭhânaṁ iṭṭhavipâkapadaṭṭhânaṁ[4] sugatisampâpakaṁ; sâvajjâniṭṭhavipâkalakkhaṇaṁ akusalaṁ avodânabhâvarasaṁ ayonisomanasîkârapadaṭṭhânaṁ duggatisampâpakaṁ; tadubhayaviparitalakkhaṇaṁ[5] abyâkataṁ avipâkârahaṁ vâ kusalâkusalapaggahena.[6]

Sadâ kusalena ca yaṁ kusalaṁ catubhûmakaṁ
muninâ vasinâ lapitaṁ lapitaṁ ṭhapitaṁ mayâ
[c] pâpâpâpesu pâpena yaṁ vuttaṁ pâpamânasaṁ
[d] pâpâpâpapahînena taṁ mayâ samudâhaṭaṁ;[7]

kriyâkriyapattivibhâgadesako
kriyâkriyâcittam avoca yaṁ jino
hitâhitânaṁ kriyâkriyato kriyâkriyaṁ [e] tantu mayâ [f] samîritan[8] ti.

[1.2] S.D.P. kamaṇḍalunodakena. [3] B.F.L. and S.D.P. have vibhajjanto. [4] B.F.L. adds yonisomanasîkârapadaṭṭhânaṁ vâ. [5] S.D.P. tadubhayaṁ viparitalakkhaṇam abyâkataṁ. [6] B.F.L.pakatena for paggahena.

[7] S.D.P. gives these stanzas as follows :—

Sadâ kusalesu kusalena ca yaṁ kusalaṁ catubhumigataṁ
muninâ vasinâ lapitaṁ lapitaṁ sakalaṁ pi mayâ
pâpâpesu pâpena yaṁ vuttaṁ pâpamânasaṁ
pâpaṁ pâpahinena taṁ mayâ samudâhaṭaṁ.

B.F.L. has "lapitaṁ bhâsitaṁ" for "lapitaṁ lapitaṁ" and "bhummikaṁ" for "bhûmakaṁ."

[8] S.D.P. has—

Kriyâkriyâpattivibhâgadesako
kriyâkiriyâcittam avoca yaṁ jino
hitâhitânaṁ kriyâkiriyato
kriyâkiriyaṁ tantu mayâ smiritan.

Ettâvatâ ekavîsatividhaṁ kusalaṁ, dvâdasavidhaṁ akusalaṁ, chatiṁsavidhaṁ[1] vipâkaṁ, vîsatividhaṁ kriyâcittan ti vatvâ saddhammaṁ desesi.[2]

Ghoso Abhidhammamâtikaṁ sutvâ pi muyhitvâ vadati—"Bhante tuyhaṁ manto ko nâmâ" ti.

"Tâta ayaṁ Buddhamanto nâmâ" ti.

So âha—"Buddhamanto nâma gahaṭṭhena[3] mâdisena sikkhitabbo" ti.

So âha—"Buddhamanto nâma mâdisena pabbajitena sikkhitabbo;[4] kasmâ gahaṭṭhassa aparisuddhattâ bahupalibodhattâ câ" ti.

Athekasmiṁ divase Ghoso tîsu vedesu ṭhânaṭhânaṁ sallakkhetvâ âdimajjhaṁ passitvâ va no antaṁ passatî ti cintetvâ udânaṁ udânesi—

Buddhamanto nâma anaggho, Buddhamanto me pi ruccati;
Buddhamantam âgamma sabbadukkhâ pamuccan ti.

Cintetvâ ca pana mâtapitaro vanditvâ pabbajjaṁ yâci. So[5] tehi paṭikkhitto ca punappunaṁ yâcitvâ puna âha—"Tâta ahaṁ mahâtherassa santike pabbajitvâ Buddhamantaṁ pariyâpuṇitvâ manasi vâcuggataṁ katvâ vibbhamitvâ punâgatomhî[6]" ti.

Atha mâtapitaro saha pûjâya taṁ[7] gahetvâ mahâtherassa upassayaṁ netvâ paṭivedesuṁ—"Bhante ayan te nettâ; tava santike pabbajitukâmo; taṁ pabbâjethâ"[8] ti.

Tadâ so tassa kesamassuṁ ohâretvâ allacandanacuṇṇehi gihigandhaṁ jhâpetvâ setavatthaṁ nivâsetvâ tacakammaṭṭhânaṁ datvâ pabbajesi.

"Bhante tacakammaṭṭhânaṁ nâma kataman" ti.

"Kesâ lomâ nakhâ dantâ taco" ti âha. "Api ca tacakammaṭṭhânaṁ[9] nâma sabbabuddhehi avijahitaṁ; sabbabuddhâ hi nâma bodhipallaṅke nisinnâ va tacakammaṭ-

[1] P. bâttiṁsa. [2] P. and B.F.L. deseti. [3] S.D.P. gahatthena.
[4] B.F.L. adds na tumhâdisena. [5] S.D.P. so Ghoso. B.F.L. has So te asampaṭicchantâ mâtapitaro punappunam. . . . [6] B.F.L. punarâgamî.
[7] For saha pûjâya taṁ B.F.L. reads sapathe hadeyyadhammena.
[8] B.F.L. and S.D.P. pabbajehi. [9] B.F.L. tacapañcakakammaṭṭhânaṁ.

thânaṁ nâma nissâya [j] tilakkhaṇena ñânaṁ otâretvâ arahattaphalaṁ [k] sacchâkaṁsu; tenâha Bhagavâ—

Tacakammaṭṭhânaṁ nâma [1] sammâsambuddhadesitaṁ;
tacakammañca âgamma sabbadukkhâ pamuccati;
tasmâ kareyya bhâvanaṁ pavaraṁ sâdhusammataṁ; [2]
tacakammañca bhâvento [3] nibbânam adhigacchati ti.

So pi taṁ sutvâ tacakammaṭṭhânaṁ bhâvento tîsu saraṇesu patiṭṭhâya dasasîlâni [4] samâdiyitvâ pañcasu kammaṭṭhânesu tilakkhaṇaṁ uppâdetvâ [5] Buddhasâsane acalapasâdo hutvâ Buddhasâsanaṁ saddahitvâ tañca theraṁ âha—"Bhante Buddhasâsanaṁ nâma saṁsârassa antakaraṇaṁ sabbabhavesu vaṭṭadukkhavinâsakâraṇañca mayhaṁ ñâtaṁ; mayhaṁ vedâ nâma asârâ tucchâ adhuvâ; buddhâdîhi ariyehi [l] chaṭṭitabbâ" ti.

So ca pabbajjaṁ labhi. Tato paṭṭhâya so divase divase ca saṭṭhipadasahassâni vâcuggatâni katvâ ekâmâseneva tîṇi piṭakâni pariyâpuṇitvâ niṭṭhapesi. So ca tîṇi piṭakâni niṭṭhapetvâ paripuṇṇavasso va laddhupasampado hutvâ catûsu paṭisambhidâsu avihatañâṇo hoti. So ca sakalajambudîpe Buddhaghoso ti nâmena pâkaṭo hoti. So ca devamanussânaṁ piyo hoti manâpo. Tenâhu porâṇâ—

Mahâbodhisamîpamhi jâto brâhmaṇakulesu
Buddhaghoso ti nâmena Buddho viya mahîtale;
pûjito naradevehi brâhmaṇehi pi pûjito
pûjito bhikkhusaṁghehi; niccaṁ labhati pûjitan ti.

iti Buddhaghosanâmatherassa pabbajitassa âcariyapajjhâyehi laddhupasampadassa dutiyaparicchedavaṇṇanâ samattâ.

[1] S.D.P. makes the first pâda "Tacakammaṁ nâma varaṁ." [2] S.D.P. and B.F.L. sârasammataṁ, in the former sâdhu being corrected to sâra. [3] B.F.L. karonto. [4] S.D.P. dasasîlaṁ. [5] S.D.P. upaṭṭhapetvâ.

CHAPTER THIRD.

HIS FATHER'S CONVERSION.

ATHEKADIVASE rahogatassa [a] paṭisallinassa cetoparivitakko udapâdi—"Mayhaṁ paññâ Buddhavacanena adhikataro udâhu upajjhâyassa adhikataro" ti. Tadâ so upajjhâyo mahâkhîṇâsavo cetasâ cetoparivitakkamaññâya—"Etarahi Buddhaghosa tava takko mayhaṁ na ruccati; yadi tvaṁ vitakkesi samaṇasâruppo nâma na hoti; khamâpehi me khippan" ti âha.

So pi upajjhâyassa vacanaṁ sutvâ bhîtacitto saṁvegapatto tañca abhiyâcitvâ—"Ayaṁ mama sâvajjo, khamatha me bhante" ti âha.

Upajjhâyo—"Yadi tvaṁ khamasi mayhaṁ tvaṁ Laṅkâdîpaṁ gantvâ Buddhavacanaṁ Sîhaḷabhâsato apanetvâ Mâgadhabhâsâya karohi; tadâhaṁ tayâ khamito bhavissâmî" ti vatvâ tuṇhî ahosi.

So âha—"Yadi tvaṁ icchasi mayhaṁ Laṅkâdîpaṁ gantuṁ icchâmi; bhante yâva pitaraṁ micchâdiṭṭhito mocessâmi tâva [b] adhivâsehî" ti; vatvâ ca pana upajjhâyaṁ âpucchitvâ attano gehaṁ gato.

Kesîbrâhmaṇo attano puttaṁ disvâ cintesi—"Idâni mama putto gihi bhavissasi; mayhaṁ puttassa mukhañca pasîdatî" ti. Tuṭṭho taṁ pucchi—"Idâni vibbhamitvâ gihi bhavissatî" ti.

So taṁ sutvâ tuṇhî ahosi. So attano vasanaṭhânaṁ gantvâ dve gabbhakuṭiyo kâretvâ upari iṭṭhakâhi chadanaṁ katvâ[1] mattikâhi limpâpetvâ va [c] badarena [d] saṅkhâretvâ[2] ekasmiṁ gabbhe anto ca bahi ca dve aggaḷâni

[1] P. and B.F.L. bhittisu.

[2] B.F.L. has "âsanaṁ pattharitvâ" for "va badarena saṅkhâretvâ."

yojetvâ aggikapâlataṇḍulodakakhîradadhisappiâdîni[1] ca ṭhapetvâ yantaṁ yojetvâ attano pitaraṁ antogabbhaṁ pavîsâpetvâ yantayuttena dvâraṁ pidahâpesi.

Kesîbrâḥmaṇo pucchi—"Tâta ahaṁ te pitâ, kasmâ evaṁ karosî" ti.

So âha—"Saccaṁ me tvaṁ pitâ asi; api ca tvaṁ micchâdiṭṭhiko Buddhasâsane apasanno asaddhakosi,[2] tasmâ evaṁ daṇḍaṁ akâsin" ti.

So—"Nâhaṁ micchâdiṭṭhikammaṁ karomi; dvâraṁ me vivarâhî" ti âha.

"Yadi tvaṁ micchâkammaṁ na karosi, 'iti pi so Bhagavâtyâdibuddhaguṇaṁ abhâsî' ti vatvâ ahaṁ dvâraṁ te vivarissâmî" ti âha; "tâta micchâdiṭṭhikammaṁ apahâya kâlaṅkate avîcimhi nippattissasî" ti vatvâ nirayabhayena pitaraṁ tajjesi. Puna ca pitaraṁ micchâdiṭṭhikammena garahanto imâyo gâthâyo abhâsi—

> **Adassane morassa [e] sikhino mañjubhâṇino**
> **kâkaṁ tattha apûjeyyuṁ [3] maṁsena ca phalena ca.**
>
> **Yadâ ca rasasampanno moro va merum âgamâ**
> **atha lâbho ca sakkâro [f] vâyasassa [g] ahâyatha.**
>
> **Yâva nuppajjati Buddho dhammarâjâ pabhaṅkaro**
> **tattha aññe apûjeyyuṁ [3] puthu samaṇabrâhmaṇe.**
>
> **Yadâ ca rasasampanno Buddho dhammam adesayi**
> **atha lâbho ca sakkâro titthiyânaṁ ahâyatha.**
>
> **Yathâ pi [h] khajjopanakâ [4] kâḷapakkhamhi rattiyâ**
> **dassayanti ca obhâsaṁ etesaṁ [5] viya sobhato.[6]**
>
> **Yadâ ca rasmisampanno [i] abbhudeti [7] pabhaṅkaro**
> **atha khajjopanakânaṁ [8] pabhâ antaradhâyati.**
>
> **Evaṁ khajjupasadisâ [9] titthiyâ pi bahû idha [10]**
> **kâḷapakkhupamâ loke dîpayanti sakaṁ guṇaṁ.**

---

[1] S.D.P. has kappala for kapâla and B.F.L. adds sakkara before khîra. [2] B.F.L. asaddho ahosi. [3] S.D.P. and P. apûjeyyuṁ. [4] So in all three MSS. [5] B.F.L. dassayati ca obhâso. [6] B.F.L. etesu viya sobhiyo. [7] P. and S.D. P. ambhareti. [8] P. and S.D.P. khajjupamasaṅghânaṁ. [9] B.F.L. khajjopanasamo. [10] B.F.L. puthû.

Yadâ ca Buddho lokamhi[1] udeti amitappabhâ
nippabhâ titthiyâ honti sûriyo khajjupamo[2] yathâ ti.

So pi tîṇi divasâni adhivâsetvâ catutthadivase attano puttena vuttaṁ Buddhaguṇaṁ anussaritvâ 'iti pi so Bhagavâtyâdîni' vâcetvâ tîsu saraṇesu anavajjapasâdo hutvâ—"Ajjatagge pâṇupetaṁ saraṇaṁ gatomhî" ti vatvâ âha—"Ayaṁ tâta Bhagavâ me satthâ, ahaṁ upâsako"[3] ti. So pi Buddhaguṇaṁ nissâya attano diṭṭhiṁ nibbindamâno sotâpattiphale patiṭṭhâti."[4]

Buddhaghoso ca dvâraṁ vivarâpetvâ attano pitaraṁ gandhodakena nhâpetvâ gandhamâlâdîhi taṁ pûjetvâ attano dosaṁ khamâpesi.

So pi sotâpannato[5] paṭṭhâya sammâsambuddhaṁ pasaṁsanto imâ gâthâyo abhâsi—

[k] Seṭṭhabhaggehi yutto yo arahanto padakkhiṇaṁ[6]
sabbadhammesu sambuddho so me satthâ dijuttamo.

Vijjâcaraṇasampanno sabbadhammassa sugato
sabbalokesu jânanto so me satthâ dijuttamo.

Anuttaro yo Bhagavâ purisânañca dammako
assânaṁ sârathi viya so me satthâ dijuttamo[7] ti.

So pana attano pituvacanaṁ sutvâ somanassacitto hutvâ "sâdhu sâdhû" ti pitaraṁ anumodi.

iti Buddhaghosena katassa micchâdiṭṭhiyâ
pitumocanupâyassa tatiya-paric-
chedavaṇṇanâ
samattâ.

[1] B.F.L. and S.D.P. lokasmiṁ. [2] S.D.P. khajjupamâ; B.F.L. khajjupabhâ. [3] Three MSS. upâsakosi. [4] S.D.P. patiṭṭhahi. [5] S.D.P. sotâpannakâlato. [6] S.D.P. araho pana dakkhiṇaṁ. [7] B.F.L. omits this stanza.

CHAPTER FOURTH.

VOYAGE TO CEYLON.

So ca taṁ attano pitaraṁ sotâpattiphale patiṭṭhapetvâ attano dosaṁ khamâpetvâ tañca âpucchitvâ upajjhâyassa santikaṁ punâgami. So upajjhâyena pesito yathâbhirantaṁ vasitvâ Laṅkâdîpagamanatthâya tañca âpucchitvâ mahâvâṇijehi sadhiṁ titthaṁ gantvâ nâvaṁ âruhitvâ pakkami. Tassa ca nikkhamanadivase yeva Buddhadattamahâthero pi Laṅkâdîpato nikkhamanto. "Puna Jambudîpam âgamâmâ" ti cintetvâ saha vâṇijehi nâvaṁ âruhitvâ âgato va hoti.

Buddhaghoso pi tîṇi divasâni mahâsamudde nâvâya pakkanto yeva hoti. Buddhadatto pi tîṇi divasâni mahâsamudde nâvâya punâgami yeva. Sakkâdînaṁ devânaṁ ânubhâvena dvinnaṁ therânaṁ dve nâvâ ekato saṅghaṭṭitâ va hutvâ aṭṭhaṁsu.

Atha vâṇijâ naṁ disvâ bhîtacittâ va aññamaññaṁ passiṁsu. Dvîsu theresu Buddhaghoso bahi nikkhamanto yeva attano sahâyavâṇije bhîtacitte disvâ apare vâṇije pucchi—"Bhonto tumhâkaṁ nâvâya ko nu pabbajito âgato atthî" ti.

Buddhadattassa pana sahâyavâṇijâ pi "Buddhadatto atthî" ti vadiṁsu.[1]

Taṁ sutvâ Buddhadatto bahi nikkhamitvâ theraṁ passitvâ ativiya tuṭṭho pucchi—"Tuvaṁ âvuso kinnâmosî" ti.

So âha "Buddhaghoso" ti.

"Kahaṁ gatosî" ti.

"Laṅkâdîpaṁ ahaṁ gatomhi bhante" ti.

"Kimatthâya gatosî" ti.

[1] B.F.L. omits this sentence, which is somewhat inaccurately expressed in the two other MSS., both leaving out "Buddhadatto" before "atthî" ti.

"Buddhasâsanaṁ Sîhaḷabhâsâya ṭhapitaṁ; taṁ parivattetvâ Mâgadhabhâsâya ṭhapetuṁ[1] gatomhî" ti.

So âha "Buddhasâsanaṁ parivattetvâ Mâgadhabhâsâya likhitvâ âgamanatthâya pesito[2] ahañca Jinâlaṅkâradantadhâtubodhivaṁsaganthe[3] yeva bandhâmi, na aṭṭhakathâṭikâyo;[4] yadi bhavaṁ sâsanaṁ Sîhaḷabhâsâya parivattetvâ Mâgadhabhâsâya karosi tiṇṇaṁ piṭakânaṁ aṭṭhakathâṭikâyo karohî" ti Buddhaghosaṁ ârâdhetvâ Sakkena devânam indena attano dinnaṁ [a]haritakiṁ[5] ayamayaṁ daṇḍalekhanañca sîlañca tassa datvâ[6] anumodi. So ca—"Yadâ te cakkhurogo vâ [b]piṭṭhirujjanaṁ vâ uppajjati tadâ idaṁ haritakiṁ sîlâyaṁ [c]pisetvâ rujjanaṭṭhâne limpetvâ tuyhaṁ rogo vûpasamatî" ti [d]tassa ânubhâvaṁ dassetvâ tassa adâsi. So [e]Jinâlaṅkâre tâva âdimhi—

> Sukhañca dukkhaṁ samâtâyupekkhaṁ
> nevicchi yo kâmam akâmanîtaṁ
> asaṅkhâtaṁsaṅkhâtasambhavaṁbhavaṁ
> hitvâ gato taṁ sugataṁ namâmî ti.

namakâragâthaṁ sutvâ âha—"Bhante tava gantho ativiya vilâsena[7] racito; pacchâ kulaputtehi na sakkâ atthaṁ jânituṁ, bâlapurisehi dubbiññeyyo"[8] ti.

"Âvuso Buddhaghosa ahaṁ tayâ pubbe Laṅkâdîpe Bhagavato sâsanaṁ kâtuṁ[9] âgatomhî" ti vatvâ "Ahaṁ appâyuko, na cîraṁ jîvâmi; tasmâ na sakkomi sâsanaṁ kâtuṁ;[9] tvaṁ yeva sâdhu karohî" ti âha.

Evaṁ pariyattisâsane dvinnaṁ therânaṁ vacanapariyosâne vâṇijânaṁ dve nâvâ sayameva muñcitvâ gatâ. Tâsu Buddhaghosassa nâvâ Laṅkâdîpâbhimukhâ hutvâ gatâ hoti; Buddhadattassa pana nâvâ Jambudîpâbhimukhâ hutvâ gatâ. Atha Buddhadatto saha vâṇijehi Jambudîpaṁ patto.

[1] S. D. P. kathetuṁ.
[2] B.F.L. likkhituṁ pesito for likhitvâ âgamanatthâya pesito.
[3] S.D.P. ganthaṁ. [4] B.F.L. omits ṭikâ. [5] P. and B.F.L. haritakaṁ.
[6] B.F.L. omits anumodi, So ca. [7] P. ativiya lâbhena; B.F.L. ativisâlena.
[8] S.D.P. duviññeyyo. B.F.L. has gaṇikâ viya alaṅkârabi châdeti instead of bâlapurisehi dubbiññeyyo. [9] S.D.P. karituṁ.

Katipâhaṁ vasitvâ samaṇadhammaṁ pûretvâ kâlaṁ katvâ Tusîtapure[1] nibbatti. Vâṇijâ pana therassa 'catupaccayanissandena kâlaṁ katvâ Tâvatiṁsabhavane nibbatiṁsu. Buddhaghoso pi vâṇijehi saddhiṁ Laṅkâdîpaṁ patto. Dvijaṭhânatitthassa samîpe nâvaṁ ṭhapetvâ vasi.

iti Buddhaghosassa Laṅkâdîpaṁ saṁ-
pattagamanacatutthaparic-
chedavaṇṇanâ
samattâ.

[1] S.D.P. Tûssitapûre.

CHAPTER FIFTH.

BUDDHAGHOSA AS A WITNESS.

TASMIṀ katipâhaṁ vasante yeva anto-Laṅkâdîpe brâhmaṇânaṁ dve dâsiyo ghaṭam âdâya udakaṁ osiñcituṁ gatâ.[1] Dvîsu[2] ekabrâhmaṇadâsî purato titthagatodakaṁ [a] osiñcitvâ ârohati. Tassâ pi ârohanakâle yeva ekâ brâhmaṇadâsî turitaturitâ va pacchato tasmiṁ titthe gatâ yeva. Tassâ ghaṭena Orohanabrâhmaṇadâsiyâ ghaṭo paṭihaññamâno va bhijji.

Sâ ghaṭabhinnâ brâhmaṇadâsî taṁ kujjhitvâ paribhâsitvâ—"Dâsiputtosi, gaṇikâya puttosi; goṇo viya na jânâsî" ti atirekatarassa akkosanavatthûhi[3] taṁ akkosi.

Itarâ pi attano paribhâsaṁ sutvâ va kuddhâ hutvâ tatheva paribhâsi taṁ akkocchi.[4] Muhuttaṁ yeva sâ pi akkosanaparibhâsanakathâ dvîhi dâsîhi kathitvâ ativiya [b] aṅgatarâ[5] bhâṇavâramattaṁ[6] va ahosi.

Buddhaghoso taṁ sutvâ cintesi—"Idha añño koci natthi; imâyo dâsiyo aññamaññaṁ paribhâsitvâ maṁ sakkhiṁ katvâ attano sâmikânaṁ ârocessanti; atha maṁ pucchissanti; pucchanakâle dassâmî" ti dvinnaṁ paribhâsanavacanaṁ attano potthake likhitvâ ṭhapesi—"Tâsu ekâ îdisaṁ nâma paribhâsaṁ karoti; aparâ îdisaṁ nâma paribhâsan" ti.

Tâ pi cîrataraṁ aññamaññaṁ atiparibhâsanena kilantamukhâ gehaṁ gantvâ attano sâmikânaṁ ârocesuṁ.

So pana ghaṭabhinnâya dâsiyâ sâmiko asantuṭṭho itarâya

[1] S.D.P. ghaṭâya udakaṁ osiñcitvâuṁ gatâ. B.F.L. ghaṭe âdâya udakatthâya âgatâ. [2] B.F.L. Tâsu. [3] B.F.L. atirekataraṁ dasahi akkosavatthûhi. [4] B.F.L. paribhâsati, akkosati. [5] B.F.L. siṅghatarâ; P. asaṅgatarâ; S.D.P. aṅgatarâ. [6] B.F.L. bhâṇavâramattâ.

sâmikena kalahaṁ katvâ rañño vinicchayaṭhânaṁ[1] gantvâ taṁ âcikkhi.

Râjâ vinicchitvâ aṭṭaṁ chindituṁ asamattho—"Ko nâma tumhâkaṁ sakkhî" ti pucchi.

Dvîsu ekâ—"Eko deva âgantuko [c]saṁghadaṇḍako tithe atthi; so mayhaṁ sakkhî" ti râjânaṁ saññâpesi.

Itarâ pi[2] tameva theraṁ uddisitvâ tatheva râjânaṁ saññâpesi.

Atha râjâ taṁ sutvâ theraṁ pucchâpetuṁ dûtaṁ[3] pesesi.

Buddhaghoso pi "Dvinnaṁ brâhmaṇitthînaṁ[4] paribhâsanakathâ mayâ ekantena sutâ; api ca mayaṁ pabbajitâ nâma na sallakkhemâ"[5] ti avatvâ[6] attanâ likhitaparibhâsanalañjanapotthakaṁ dûtassa hatthe datvâ "Tâta idameva lañjanapotthakaṁ rañño dassehî" ti âha.

Dûto taṁ gahetvâ rañño dassesi. Râjâ taṁ vâcâpetvâ dve dâsiyo pucchi—"Are bhotiyo îdisâ nâma paribhâsanâ tumhehi saccaṁ kathitâ" ti.[7]

Tâ pi[8] "Saccaṁ devâ" ti âhaṁsu.

Râjâ âha "Garubhâradhâriko nâma agarubhâradhârikena vajjetabbo" ti; vatvâ ca pana abhinnaghaṭâya brâhmaṇadâsiyâ daṇḍaṁ dâpesi.

Atha so râjâ taṁ theraṁ daṭṭhukâmo brâhmaṇe pucchi—"So tâdiso [d]javanapañño kahaṁ vasatî" ti.

Brâhmaṇâ micchâdiṭṭhikâ therassa guṇaṁ maccharino—"Deva ayaṁ saṅghadaṇḍako vâṇijjatthâya âgato; tumhehi daṭṭhuṁ ananurûpo" ti âhaṁsu.

Râjâ taṁ sutvâ therassa guṇe pasîditvâ pasaṁsanto dve gâthâyo abhâsi—

> Samaṇesu ca sabbesu Laṅkâdîpe bahûsu pi
> tâdiso samaṇo nâma na diṭṭhapubbo yo idha.

---

[1] S.D.P. and P. vinicchayatabbaṭṭhânaṁ ; P. vinicchayitabbaṭhânaṁ
[2] S.D.P. and P. Ekâ pana. [3] S.D.P. dûte. [4] B.F.L. brâhmaṇidâsînaṁ. [5] B.F.L. sakkhimhâ. [6] B.F.L. vatvâ. [7] P. "Îdisaṁ nâma paribhâsanaṁ tumhehi kathitaṁ saccaṁ kathitan" ti. [8] S.D.P. and P. dve dâsiyo instead of tâ pi.

**Tâdisaṁ sîlasampannaṁ javañâṇaṁ[1] mahâtapaṁ
yo ca pûjeti mâneti saggaṁ so upagacchati[2] ti.**

Evaṁ dvîhi gâthâhi Buddhaghosassa guṇaṁ vatvâ râjâ tuṇhî ahosi.

iti Buddhaghosena kathitassa attano
paññâya dvinnaṁ brâhmaṇadâsî-
naṁ sakkhibhâvassa pañcama-
paricchedavaṇṇanâ
samattâ.

[1] S.D.P. javaññâṇaṁ. [2] S.D.P. saggaṁ so ca upajjhagâ.

CHAPTER SIXTH.

PERMISSION TO TRANSLATE THE SCRIPTURES.

TATO paṭṭhâya thero Laṅkâdîpavâsisaṅgharâjamahâtherassa vandanatthâya gato. So ca taṁ vanditvâ saṅgharâjamahâtherassa santike Abhidhammavinaye sikkhantânaṁ bhikkhûnaṁ pacchato ekamantaṁ nisîdi.

Athekasmiṁ divase saṅgharâjâ bhikkhûnaṁ sikkhanto Abhidhamme gaṇṭhipadaṁ patvâ tassa ca gaṇṭhipadassa adhippâyaṁ apassitvâ ajânitvâ mûḷho hutvâ bhikkhû uyyojento antogabbhaṁ pavisitvâ taṁ gaṇṭhipadaṁ vicâretvâ nisîdi.

Tassa pana pavîsanakâle yeva Buddhaghoso Abhidhamme gaṇṭhipadaṁ ajânantaṁ mahâtheraṁ ñatvâ uṭṭhâyâsanâ upasseyyaphalake[1] gaṇṭhipadassa atthañca adhippâyañca likhitvâ ṭhapetvâ va attano nâvaṁ gato.

Tassa pana gaṇṭhipadassa atthaṁ punappunaṁ cintentassa atthañca adhippâyañca ajânitvâ gabbhato nikkhamantassa nisinnakâle[2] yeva taṁ akkharaṁ pâkaṭaṁ ahosi. Disvâ ca pana tâpase pucchi—"Idaṁ akkharaṁ nâma kena likkhitan" ti.

Tâpasâ âhaṁsu—"Bhante âgantukena bhikkhunâ taṁ likkhitaṁ bhavissatî" ti.

"So kuhiṁ gato" ti vatvâ "tumhe pariyesitvâ tam gahetvâ mayhaṁ dassethâ" ti tâpase âṇâpesi.

Tâpasâ pariyesamânâ passitvâ taṁ ârâdhetvâ saṅgharâjassa dassesuṁ.

So pi saṅgharâjâ "Idaṁ kira akkharaṁ nâma tayâ likhitan" ti pucchitvâ "âma bhante" ti vutte "Tena hi

[1] P. upasye ; B.F.L. apassena ; S.D.P. upasye and upassane.
[2] P. and S.D.P. nisîdanakâle.

tayâ tîhi piṭakehi bhikkhusaṅgho sikkhitabbo" ti bhikkhusaṅghassa [b] paṭiniyyâdeti.[1]

Buddhaghoso pi taṁ paṭikkhipi—"Nâhaṁ bhante bhikkhusaṅghe sikkhanatthâya Jambudîpato Laṅkâdîpaṁ âgato Buddhasâsanaṁ pana Sîhaḷabhâsâya parivattetvâ Mâgadhabhâsâya likhanatthâya âgato" ti attano âgatakâraṇaṁ tassa ârocesi.[2]

So taṁ sutvâ ativiya tuṭṭho "Yadi 'sâsanaṁ Mâgadhabhâsâya likhissâmî' ti vatvâ âgatosi.

[c] sîle patiṭṭhâya naro sapañño
cittaṁ paññañca bhâvayaṁ
âtâpî nipako bhikkhu
ko imaṁ vijaṭaye jaṭan ti.

Bhagavatâ vuttagâthâya tîṇi piṭakâni yojetvâ amhâkaṁ dassehî" ti âha.

So "Sâdhû" ti sampaṭicchitvâ attano vasanaṭhânaṁ gato.

Tasmiṁ divase sunakkhattena vaḍḍhamânacchâyâya

sîle patiṭṭhâya naro sapañño
cittaṁ paññañca bhâvayaṁ
âtâpî nipako bhikkhu
ko imaṁ vijaṭaye jaṭan ti.

âdiṁ katvâ Visuddhimaggapakaraṇaṁ atilahukena likhi. Niṭṭhapetvâ ca pana "ṭhapessâmî" ti niddûpagato hoti.

Atha Sakko devarâjâ therena ṭhapitalikhitaṁ Visuddhimaggaṁ thenetvâ gato. Thero ca pabujjhitvâ attano

[1] The reading of this sentence in P. and S.D.P. is as follows:—"So pi saṅgharâjâ puṭṭho 'idaṁ kira akkharaṁ nâma tayâ likhitan' ti; 'âma bhante' ti âha; so puṭṭho tena puṭṭhasmiṁ 'pakatiyâ tîhi piṭakehi bhikkhusaṅghâ sikkhitabbâ' ti vatvâ bhikkhusaṅghe tassa paṭivedesi."

[2] This sentence appears as follows in P. and S.D.P.:—"Buddhaghoso pi taṁ paṭikkhipi—'Nâhaṁ bhante bhikkhusaṅghe sikkhituṁ icchâmi; Laṅkâdîpaṁ âgatomhi' ti âha; 'Kasmâ, ahaṁ pana Jambudîpavâsi; Tathâgata Buddhasâsanaṁ Sîhalabhâsato parivattitvâ Mâgadhabhâsâya likhissâmi mantâ gato.'"

pakaraṇaṁ adisvâ puna ca paraṁ Visuddhimaggapakaraṇaṁ ativiya turitaturito dîpâlokena likhi. Taṁ pi niṭṭhapetvâ attano sîse ṭhapetvâ puna niddûpagato. Sakko ca devarâjâ puna taṁ thenetvâ gato hoti. Thero kiñci supitvâ puna pabujjhitvâ taṁ na passi. Majjhimayâme sampatte yeva kira Sakko devarâjâ dutiyavâre duvidhaṁ pakaraṇaṁ thenetvâ gato.

Thero pabujjhitvâ taṁ adisvâ turitaturito puna ca paraṁ Visuddhimaggapakaraṇaṁ dîpâlokena likhi. Likhitâvasâne cîvarena bandhitvâ va supati.[1] Sakko devarâjâ purimagahite dve pakarane therassa sîse thapetvâ gato. Vibhâtâya rattiyâ pabujjhitvâ va attanâ likhite pakaraṇe devarâjena attano ussîsake[2] ṭhapite disvâ somanasso hutvâ sarîravalañjanakiccaṁ katvâ dve ganthâni âdâya attano bandhitaganthena saddhiṁ Laṅkâdîpavâsisaṅgharâjatherassa dasseti.[3]

Tîsu ganthesu kira tisatasahassanavanahutadvesahassâdhikâni dasasahassâni akkharâni yeva honti. So pi tîṇi disvâ accariyabhûto "Kasmâ tîṇi pakaraṇânî" ti pucchitvâ "Iminâ kâraṇenâ" ti vutte vimhayamâno tîṇi ganthâni vâcâpeti. Tîsu yasmiṁ padese ye nipâtopasaggâ[4] saddâ therena likhitâ tassa tasmiṁ padese te samasamâ a-vi-sadisâ likhitâ viya tiṭṭhanti. Tena samasame a-visadisasadise disvâ ativiya somanasso va tassa "Bhagavato sâsanaṁ Mâgadhabhâsâya karohî" ti anujâni. Anujânitvâ ca panassa paññâya guṇaṁ pasaṁsanto dve gâthâ abhâsi—

> Yo passatîdisaṁ paññaṁ abhinnapaṭisambhidaṁ[5]
> sabbadhammesu kosallaṁ Buddham so viya passati;
>
> tvañceva[6] ñâṇasampanno amhâkaññeva[7] seṭṭhaṅgo
> tvaññeva[8] sâsanantassa karassu munino sadâ ti.

Tato paṭṭhâya so tasmiṁ dîpe Buddhaghoso ti nâmena Laṅkâdîpe manussânaṁ pâkaṭo hoti. Tenâhu porânâ—

[1] S.D.P. supi. [2] S.D.P. usisakke; P. and B.F.L. usisagge.
[3] S.D.P. dassesi. [4] S.D.P. nipâtopasaggâdayo. [5] B.F.L. pabhinna°.
[6] S.D.P. tvaṁ yeva. [7] S.D.P. amhâkañceva.

Buddhaghoso ti nâmena pâkaṭo sabbadîpake ;
manussânaṁ sadâ seṭṭho Budho viya mahîtale ti.

iti Laṅkâdîpavâsimahâtherena aj anu-
jânitasâsanassa Buddhaghosassa
chaṭṭhamaparicchedavaṇ-
ṇanâ samattâ.

CHAPTER SEVENTH.

OBJECT ATTAINED.

So yathâbhirantaṁ vasitvâ[1] attano sâruppasenasanaṁ[2] saṅghaṁ yâci munindasâsanassa lekhanatthâya. Mahâthero therassa vasituṁ lohapâsâdaṁ dâpesi. So kira lohapâsâdo sattabhûmiko ahosi.[3] Tâsu cha bhûmiyo chahi mahâtherehi vasitâ honti. Katame cha? Eko catupârisuddhisîladharo dutiye vasati; eko dhûtaṅgadharo tatiye vasati; eko suttantadharo catutthe vasati; eko abhidhammadharo pañcame vasati; eko vinayadharo chaṭṭhe vasati; eko maggaphalatthâya tilakkhaṇabhâvanâyuttajhânadharo[4] sattame bhûmitale vasati. Pâsâdassa heṭṭhimabhûmitalâ suññâ abhikkhukâ hoti.

Buddhaghoso panassa heṭṭhimatale suññe paṭivasati. So kira dhûtaṅgadharo hoti; sabbapariyattidharo ca hoti. Vasanto ca pana Bhagavato sâsanaṁ dîpabhâsato parivattetvâ Mâgadhabhâsâya divase divase likhi.

Puna divase so pâto va piṇḍâya caranto sayaṁpatitatâlapaṇṇaṁ disvâ âdâya gocaragâmato paṭikkami. Idaṁ eva cassa vattan ti veditabbaṁ.[5]

Athekasmiṁ divase [a]tâlâruḷhakapuriso paṇḍito byatto [b]kusalattiko tassa kiriyaṁ disvâ achiddaṁ akhaṇḍakaṁ tâlapaṇṇaṁ tassa piṇḍapâtaṭhâne vikiritvâ niliyi. Thero piṇḍapâtâvasâne taṁ âdâya gato.

So tassa anugantvâ therassa likhanakiccam disvâ pasannacitto hutvâ[6] ekadivase[7] bhattapacchiṁ âdâya therassa

[1] B.F.L. viharitvâ.
[2] B.F.L. anurûpas°.
[3] B.F.L. hoti.
[4] S.D.P. tilakkhaṇabhâvanâya yutto jhânadharo.
[5] P. and S.D.P. Idameva cassa vattaṁ.
[6] P. and S.D.P. hoti.
[7] P. and S.D.P. ekadivasmhi so.

pûjesi. Thero tañca "Bho upâsaka mayhaṁ uparimatale ṭhito seṭṭhataro; tassa tava bhojanaṁ dadâhî" ti vadati.[1]

So therena anuññâto pacchiṁ âdâya uparimatale ṭhitassa mahâtherassa adâsi.

Eteneva mukhena ekabhattapacchi yâva sattamabhûmitale ṭhitassa ayyassa sampapuṇi.

So ca uparimatale ṭhito taṁ âha—"Heṭṭhimatale Buddhaghoso amhehi guṇavisiṭṭho; divase divase Buddhasâsanaṁ likhi; tasseva dadâhî" ti.[2]

So taṁ sutvâ bhattapacchiṁ âdâya sattabhûmitalâ oruyha Buddhaghosassa puna adâsi.

So "sâdhu sâdhû" ti sampaṭicchi; sampaṭicchitvâ ca pana sattakoṭṭhâsena bhâjâpetvâ cha koṭṭhâse channaṁ therânaṁ dâpesi. Idameva tassa vattaṁ. So Buddhaghoso sâsanaṁ likhanto yeva tayo mâse khepetvâ niṭṭhaṁ gato. Vuṭṭhavasso tato paṭṭhâya pavâretvâ attanâ likhitasâsanaṁ saṅgharâjassa[3] paṭivedesi.

So "sâdhu sâdhû" ti anumoditvâ ca pana tassa guṇaṁ pakâsento[4] dve gâthâyo abhâsi—

> **Sâsanaṁ nâma dullabhaṁ Buddhaseṭṭhassa bhâsitaṁ**
> **parivattânubhâvena taṁ passâma yathâsukhaṁ**
>
> **yathâ pi puriso andho samâsamaṁ na passati**
> **tathâ mayaṁ na passâma sâsanaṁ Buddhabhâsitan ti.**

Tato paṭṭhâya so pi Mahindatherena likhâpitâni ganthâni râsiṁ kârâpetvâ [6] mahâcetiyassa samîpe parisuddhaṭhâne jhâpesi. Sîhaḷabhâsâya kira Mahindatherena likhâpitâni sabbaganthâni[5] râsikatâni ubbedhena sattamajjhimahatthipiṭṭhipamaṇâni honti ti pubbâcariyâ vadantî ti amhehi sutaṁ.

Sîhalabhâsâya katânaṁ[6] sabbesaṁ ganthânaṁ jhâ-

[1] S.D.P has "So 'Tañca bho upâsaka uparitale ṭhitassa ayyassa dadâhî vadati; kasmâ ca pana vadâma upariṭhito mayhaṁ seṭṭhataro ca hoti."

[2] P. and S.D.P. So ca uparitale ṭhito taṁ âha—"Heṭṭhimatalassa Buddhaghosassa amhehi guṇavisiṭṭhassa divase divase Buddhasâsanaṁ likhantasseva dadâhî." [3] S.D.P. saṅghasseva. [4] P. and S.D.P. pakâsanto. [5] S.D.P. sabbâni ganthâni. [6] P. and S.D.P. kathitânaṁ.

panakâlato paṭṭhâya so ca attano mâtâpitûnaṁ dassanatthâya saṅghaṁ âpucchi—"Ahaṁ bhante Jambudîpaṁ gamituṁ icchâmî" ti vatvâ vâṇijehi saddhiṁ nâvaṁ ârohituṁ ârabbhi. Tassa attano nâvâbhirûhanakkhaṇe[1] yeva Sîhaḷavâsino bhikkhû [d]sakkaṭaganthe paguṇataṁ avamaññanti—"Ayaṁ thero dhi nu[2] tepiṭakaṁ Buddhasâsanaṁ jânâti maññe na sakkaṭaganthan" ti.

Tesaṁ avamaññavacanaṁ sutvâ therassa sahâyavâṇijâ tassa ârocesuṁ.

Thero taṁ sutvâ "sâdhu sâdhû" ti vatvâ Laṅkâdîpavâsino saṅgharâjamahâtherassa paṭivedesi—"Bhante sve uposathadivase puṇṇamiyaṁ ahaṁ pi sakkaṭaganthaṁ bhâsissâmi; catuparisâ mahâcetiyaṅgaṇe[3] sannipâtetû" ti. So pâto va parisâya majjhe sakkaṭaganthaṁ dassento dhammâsanaṁ[4] âruyha ṭhatvâ sakkaṭaganthena[5] imâ gâthâyo [e]abhâsi—

Cattâro kira acchariyâ abbhutadhammâ Buddhaghose santi.[6] Katame cattâro? Sace bhikkhuparisâ Buddhaghosadassanâya upasṅkamati dassanenassa attamanâ hoti.[7] Tatra ce Buddhaghoso dhammaṁ bhâsati bhâsitena pissa attamanâ hoti. Atittâ ca bhikkhuparisâ hoti atha kho Buddhaghoso tuṇhî hoti. Sace bhikkhuṇîparisâ upâsakaparisâ upâsikâparisâ Buddhaghosadassanâya upasaṅkamati dassanena pissa attamanâ hoti; tatra ce Buddhaghoso dhammaṁ bhâsati bhâsitena pissa attamanâ hoti. Atittâ va hoti atha kho Buddhaghos tuṇhî hotî ti evaṁ cattâro acchariyâ abbhutadhammâ Buddhaghose santi[8] âyasmante Ânande viya, tasmâ Buddhaghosassa desanâkâle yeva catasso parisâ attano attano vatthaceḷakamuttâhâravala-

[1] P. and S.D.P. nâvaṁ gatakkhaṇe.
[2] B.F.L. kinnu for dhi nu.
[3] S.D.P. mahâcetiyassa santike.
[4] P. and S.D.P. dhammadesanaṭhânaṁ.
[5] Two texts ganthe.
[6] B. F. L. uppajjanti.
[7] B.F.L. uses the plural verb with parisâ in this and the following sentences, and tattha for tattra.
[8] P. and S.D.P. have the following construction after santi—cattâro acchariyâ abbhutadhammâ viya ayasmante Ânande santi ti tasmâ, &c.

yâdîni muñcitvâ dhammapûjâya[1] therassa pâdamûle vikariṁsu. Vatthâdîni pana pûjâbhaṇḍâni kira sattahatthamajjhimahatthipiṭṭhipamâṇâni[2] honti.

So pana[3] tâni anapekkho va hutvâ dhammâsanato[4] oruyha saṅghaṁ vanditvâ mahallakaṁ mahâtheraṁ âpucchitvâ vâṇijehi saddhiṁ nâvaṁ âruyha Jambudîpâbhimukho pâyâsi. Tassa ca gatakâle yeva yâcakavaṇibbakasamaṇabrâhmaṇâdayo manussâ tâni therassa dhammapûjabhaṇḍâni[5] yathâruciṁ yeva gahetvâ pakkamiṁsu.

iti Buddhaghosanâmatherena attanâ paguṇasakkaṭaganthena kathitadhammadesanâya sattamaparicchedavaṇṇanâ samattâ.

[1] B.F.L. pûjento. [2] P. and S.D.P. omit piṭṭhi.
[3] P and S.D.P. pi. [4] P. and S.D.P. dhammadesanaṭṭhânato.
[5] P. and S.D.P. pûjâni bhaṇḍâni.

CHAPTER EIGHTH.

RETURN TO INDIA.

THERO Sakkaṭaganthe attano paṭubhâvaṁ pakâsetvâ Jambudîpâbhimukho va hutvâ samuddamajjhe âgacchanto yeva vâṇije anusâsanto dve gâthâyo abhâsi—

> Yathâ [a] mayupanissâya nâvaṁ gacchâma aṇṇave
> nâvâ ca amhe nissâya titthappattâ bhavissati
> . aggatitthaṁ patiṭṭhâya paññânâvupanissâya
> puññanâvupanissâma amhe sagge sukhâvahâ ti.

So titthappatto attano sahâyavâṇije âpucchitvâ attano pattacîvaram âdâya upajjhâyassa santikaṁ gato. Pariyattisaṅkhâtassa Buddhasâsanassa attanâ likhitakammaṁ âcikkhi; âcikkhitvâ ca pana upajjhâyadaṇḍakammaṁ mocetvâ attano dosaṁ khamâpetvâ taṁ vanditvâ âpucchitvâ va mâtâpitûnaṁ santikaṁ gato hoti.

Mâtâpitaro pissa attano puttaṁ disvâ vanditvâ paṇîtena âhârena taṁ parivisitvâ tassa dosaṁ khamâpetvâ attano kâlabhâvaṁ ñatvâ maraṇâsannakâle Buddhaguṇaṁ anussaritvâ Tusîtapure nibbattitvâ kanakavimâne paṭivasanti.[1] Tesaṁ pi dâsakammakarâdînaṁ brâhmaṇânaṁ keci therassa ovâde ṭhatvâ kâlaṁ katvâ devaloke nibbattiṁsu; keci yathâkammaṁ gati[2] ahesuṁ.[3]

Thero pana[4] tiṇṇaṁ ratanânaṁ attano paṇâmavacanaṁ dassetvâ tesu sâdhujanânaṁ pâmojjanatthâya "evaṁ pi

[1] B. Mâtapitaro pissa attano puttaṁ disvâ vanditvâ paṇîtena âhârena parivisiṁsu. Te attano nissâya micchâdiṭṭhiṁ pajahitvâ sammaditthiṁ dânâdipuññaṁ katvâ âyutapariyosâne kâlaṅ katvâ tusîtapure nibbattiṁsu.

[2] So in P. and S.D.P.

[3] The following reading occurs in B.F.L.—Tesaṁ pi dâsakammakarâdayo therassa ovâde ṭhatvâ kâlaṁ katvâ yebhûyyena devaloke nibbattiṁsu.

[4] P. and S.D.P. so ca.

tiṇṇaṁ ratanânaṁ îdiso nâma paṇâmo tumhehi kâtabbo"[1] ti vuccamâno viya[2] ratanattayassa[3] sarûpaṁ dassento âha—

Yo Bhagavâ visuddhakhandasantâno[4]
yo va so buddho ti [b] niyamâgato
dhammo nâma Bhagavatâ desito
navavidho lokuttaradhammo.

Piṭakato tîṇi piṭakâni—vinayapiṭakaṁ, suttantapiṭakaṁ, abhidhammapiṭakan ti; nikâyato pañcanikâyâni—dîghanikâyo, majjhimanikâyo, saṁyuttanikâyo, aṅguttaranikâyo, khuddakanikâyo ti; aṅgato navaṅgâni—suttaṁ, geyyaṁ, gâthâ, veyyâkaraṇaṁ, udânaṁ, itivuttakaṁ, jâtakaṁ, abbhûtadhammaṁ, vedallan ti; dhammakhandhato caturâsîti dhammakhandhasahassâni; abhidhamme cattâri dasasahassâni dvisahassadhammakhandhâ; vinaye dvâdasasahassâni ekasahassadhammakhandhâ ca; suttante dvâdasasahassâni ekasahassadhammakhandhâ câ ti; saṅgho cattâro maggaṭṭhâ cattâro phalaṭṭhâ câ ti aṭṭhannaṁ ariyânaṁ samûho.[5]

Iti ratanattayassa sarûpaṁ dassetvâ attano paṇâmañca pakâsento imaṁ gâthaṁ âha—

Buddhe dhamme ca saṅghe ca kato eko pi añjalî
pahomi bhavadukkhaggiṁ nibbâpetuṁ asesato ti.

So ca ratanattayassa paṇâmavâsane Bhagavato sâsanassa dûsanatthâya[6] katakiccânaṁ dussîlânaṁ sîlarakkhane asikkhitacittânaṁ[7] jîvitatthâya kaṭakuhakânaṁ kammañca pakâsento imâ gâthâyo abhâsi—

Yathâ pi hi migindassa sîhassa migarâjino
tassa maṁsaṁ na khâdanti [c] siṅgâlâ sunakhâdhammâ,
Sarîre samuppannâ va kimiyo maṁsabhojanâ
sîhamaṁsâni khâdanti na aññe sâpadâ migâ,

---

[1] P. and S.D.P. kato. [2] P. and S.D.P. only vatvâ for vuccamâno viya. [3] S.D.P. ratanattayânaṁ. [4] P. and S.D.P. visuddhikh°.
[5] This last sentence saṅgho—samûho is omitted in P. and S.D.P.
[6] B.F.L. dassanatthâya. [7] B.F.L. susikkhita°. S.D.P. has asikkhitasikkhânaṁ.

tatheva sakyasîhassa nibbûtassa pi sâsane
na dûsayanti saddhammaṁ iddhipattâ pi titthiyâ.
Ime va pâpabhikkhû ye muṇḍâ saṅghâṭipârutâ
te dûsayanti saddhammaṁ sammasambuddhadesitan ti.

Iti Bhagavato sâsanassa dûsanatthâya katakiccânaṁ pâpabhikkhûnaṁ yeva kammaṁ[1] pakâsanâvasâne puna pi sabbesañca sattânaṁ rattidivesu pavattaânâpânâni[2] dassento imaṁ gâthaṁ âha—

Divâ satasahassâni aṭṭhasatâdhikâni ca
rattiñceva tathâ eva [d] ânâpânaṁ pavattattî ti.

Dassetvâ ca pana attano maraṇamañce nisinno âyusaṅkhâraṁ vicârento[3] appâyukabhâvaṁ[4] ñatvâ upajjhâyaṁ vanditvâ tañca âpucchitvâ mahâbodhim[5] gantvâ mahâbodhirukkhe sabbavattâdîni pûjupakâraṇâni katvâ mahâbodhirukkhaṁ pasaṁsanto dve gâthâ abhâsi—

Bodhiṁ nissâya sambuddho sambuddho [e] dvipaduttamo
bodhipatto ca so hoti [f] Mârasenapamaddanâ;

yo bodhiṁ âdaraṁ katvâ pûjâya abhipûjayi
so ca Buddhaṁ viya pûjeti sabbadukkhâ [g] pamuñcaso[6] ti.

Iti pasaṁsitvâ so ca ekantena attano kâlaṁ ñatvâ "maraṇaṁ nâma tividhaṁ—samucchedamaraṇaṁ, [h] khaṇikamaraṇaṁ, samutimaraṇan ti; tattha samucchedamaraṇaṁ nâma khîṇâsavassa kâlaṁ, khaṇikamaraṇaṁ nâma anantaruppajjananiruddhânaṁ bhavaṅgâdivîthicittânaṁ [i] kâlaṁ; samutimaraṇaṁ nâma sabbesaṁ sattânaṁ kâlan" ti ñatvâ "Tesu mayhaṁ samutimaraṇena bhavitabban" ti cintesi. Cintetvâ ca pana maraṇadivase Buddhaguṇena saddhiṁ attano sîlaṁ anussaramâno kâlaṁ

1 P. and S.D.P kammassa.
2 Pavatta does not occur in P. and S.D.P.
3 P. and S.D.P. vicâretvâ.
4 P. and S.D.P. attano kâlaṁ.
5 P. and S.D.P. Mahâbodhisantikaṁ.
6 The reading of this line in B.F.L. is :—So ca Buddhañca pûjeti sabbadukkhâ pamuccaye.

katvâ Tusîtapure nibbattitvâ dvâdasayojanike kanakavimâne devaccharasahassapirivârâ saddhiṁ paṭivasati.

Yadâ Metteyyo bodhisatto idha manussaloke sabbaññutapatto hessati tadâ so ca tassa sâvako bhavissati aggo ca seṭṭho ca Metteyyassa Bhavagato sabbadhammesu appaṭihatena attano ñâṇavasena. So ca sattakkhatuṁ Metteyyena Bhagavatâ etadagge ṭhapito bhavissati—"Mama sâvakânaṁ dhammavinayadharânaṁ bahussutânaṁ ñâṇagatînaṁ ñâṇadharânaṁ yadidaṁ Buddhaghoso" ti.

Tasmiṁ Buddhaghose pana there kâlaṅkate yevassa kaḷeverajhâpanatthâya samaṇabrâhmaṇâdayo sabbe devamanussâ candanarukkhehi citakaṁ kârâpetvâ ratanacittakâni agghiyâni ussâpetvâ tassa kaḷevaraṁ candanarukkhacitake saha suvaṇṇamañcena[1] pakkhipitvâ sâdarena jhâpayiṁsu. Tassa kaḷeverajhâpitâvasâne brâhmaṇâdayo manussâ dhâtuyo gahetvâ mahâbodhisamîpe yeva suddhesu bhûmipadesu nidahitvâ[2] thûpaṁ kârayiṁsu. Te pi sabbe therassa guṇe pasâdetvâ iminâ[3] pûjânissandena kâlaṅkatvâ devalokesu uppajjitvâ yathâkammaṁ dibbasampattiyo anubhavantî[4] ti. Etasseva Tusîtapure vasantassa therassa pana kâlato paṭṭhâya[5] pubbâcariyâ duppaññe puggale attânaṁ pasaṁsante "paññavantamhâ" ti maññante garahantâ tisso gâthâyo âhaṁsu—

Kâlaṅkate Buddhaghose[6] "kavimhâ" ti bahûtarâ
dupaññâ bâlajanâ pi cintayiṁsu punappunaṁ.

Buddhaghose patiṭṭhante paññavantâ pi ye janâ
tesaṁ paññapabhâ natthi Râhumukhe va candimâ.

Tasmâ jaheyya medhâvî "paññavâ" ti pasaṁsanaṁ;[7]
attânaṁ saṁyamaṁ katvâ so sukhaṁ[8] na vihâyatî ti.

---

[1] P. suvaṇṇamañcavasena; S.D.P. °mañcasena. [2] P. and S.D.P. nidahiṁsu, omitting thûpaṁ kârayiṁsu. [3] P. and S.D.P. therassa.
[4] P. and S.D.P. dibbasampattiṁ abhibhavantî. [5] B.F.L. has evaṁ therassa anantarato paṭṭhâya.
[6] P. and S.D.P. have Saṅghate Buddhaghose pi. [7] P. and S.D.P. pasaṁsane. [8] All MSS. sukhâ.

iti ettâvatâ Mahâmaṅgalanâmena ekena
therena pubbâcariyânaṁ santikâ
yathâpariyattiṁ paññâya
racitassa javanahâsatikkhanibbedhika-
paññâsampanassa Buddhaghosasseva
nâma mahâtherassa nidânassa
aṭṭhamaparicchedavaṇṇa-
nâ samattâ.

AUTHOR'S ASPIRATION.

BUDDHAGHOSASSA nidânaṁ evaṁ taṁ racitaṁ mayâ
nidânassa racanena paññavâ homi sabbadâ.

Labheyyañca ahaṁ tassa Metteyyasamâgamaṁ
Metteyyo nâma sambuddho târeti janataṁ bahuṁ.

Yadâ Metteyyataṁ patto dhâreyyaṁ piṭakattayaṁ
tadâhaṁ paññavâ homi Metteyyaupasantike ti.

NOTES.

CHAPTER FIRST.

[a] Râjâ].—Sosaṅkama is the name of this king given in *Cullaganthavaṁsa.*

[b] Tihetuka]—*i.e.*, by reason of *amoha, adosa,* and *alobha.* "Tihetukâni ti alobhâdosâmohavasena tihetukâni."—*Saṅkhepavaṇṇanâṭîkâ.*

[c] Bahupayâso] = bahu + upa + âyâso (*Sk.* âyâsaka), "exceedingly vexatious," "most wearisome."

[d] Nipphattiṁ pâpuṇi].—*Cf.* Nâgasena's early career in *Milindapañha* with that of Buddhaghosa.

[e] Bissanukhandhe].—"In the place sacred to Vishṇu." This most likely represents the *Sk.* Vishṇukrânte, "On the sacred seat of Vishṇu," *krânte* being the sacred grass which is woven into a mat or cushion.

[f] Mâsaṁ].—"A bean," "a kind of pulse" (*Sk.* mâsha).

[g] Bissanu].—The name of the god as well as of a legume. Cf. *Sk.* vishṇukanda. There seems to be a reference here to the "advaita" system of philosophy, *i.e.* non-dualism, *mâso* and *bissanu* (Vishṇu) being taken as pantheistically or spiritually identical.

[h] Apaṭibhânâ].—"Mum," "silent."

[i] Palobheti].—"To coax," "to win over by artifice" (*Sk.* pra + √lubh, "to entice").

[j] Uttânaṁ katvâ].—"Having solved," "having elucidated."

CHAPTER SECOND.

[a] Vâcuggatâni].—"Got by heart."

[b] Âmasitvâ].—"Having reflected upon," literally "touched upon."

[c] Pâpâpâpesu pâpena] = pâpa + apâpesu pâpena. A variant reading is "pâpa + apâpe + supâpena;" in both cases pâpena = *Sk.* prâpena instead of prâpas, "arriving at," "attainment."

[d] Pâpâpâpapahinena] = pâpa + apâpa + pahînena.

[e] Samudâhaṭaṁ].—This is equivalent to the *Sk.* samudâhṛitaṁ, "brought together," "expressed."

[f] Tantu] = taṁ pi, taṁ referring to kriyâkriyacittaṁ. Here akiriyaṁ

is used in the metaphysical meaning of "what does not produce *kusala* or *akusala*." Hence it is a synonym for "Nirvâṇa."

[g] Samiritaṁ].—"Said," "declared." In *Sk.* we have samîrayati, "to utter."

[h] Ettâvatâ].—The enumeration in *Abhidhammatthasaṅgaha* is as follows:—

Dvâdasâkusalânevaṁ kusalânekavîsati
chattiṁseva vipâkâni kriyacittâni vîsati.

[i] Vibbhamati].—Metaphorically "to give up the priesthood," "to turn layman."

[j] Tilakkhaṇena].—The reference is to *anicca*, *dukkha*, and *anatta*.

[k] Sacchâkaṁsu].—Aor. of sacchikaroti, "to realise," "to come face to face with." Sacchâ = *Sk.* sâkshât, "by means of eyes" (*Pali*, sa + akkha + to). "*Tisso vijjâ sacchâkâsi*," "he realised the three kinds of knowledge."—*Puṇṇovâdasuttaṁ*.

[l] Chaṭṭitabbâ] = chaḍḍitabbâ, qualifying vedâ.

CHAPTER THIRD

[a] Paṭisallinassa].—Supply "Buddhaghosassa," "while Buddhaghosa was by himself." Paṭisallina, and not paṭisalliṇa, is the usual reading in Bur. MSS. (*Sk.* prati + sam + √li, "to hide," + na.)

[b] Adhivâsehi].—"Bear with," "suffer."

[c] Badarena] ≐ padarena, "with planking."

[d] Sankhâretvâ].—"Having constructed," "having strengthened" (?).

[e] Sikhino].—Gen. of sikhî, "having a crest," from sikhâ, "a crest."

[f] Vâyasassa] = kâkassa.

[g] Ahâyathâ].—3rd sing. imperfect of hâyati, "to be lost."

[h] Khajjopanaka].—"A firefly." If not a mistake for *khajjopâṇaka*, it would appear to be formed from a verb *khajjopeti*, "to shine;" *khajjopana*, "shining;" *khajjopanaka*, "the little thing that shines." *Khajjo* is a contraction of *khajjota* (*Sk.* khadyota) and furnishes the base *khajja*.

[i] Abbhudeti].—"To rise" (abhi + ud + eti) = abbhareti.

[j] Nhâpetvâ].—This is the usual form in Bur. MSS. for nahâpetvâ.

[k] Seṭṭhabhâggehi].—Literally, "with exalted fractures." The destruction of *kilesa* is referred to.

CHAPTER FOURTH

[a] Haritakî].—The fruit of the myrobolan. The *Sk.* has *haritakî* as well as *haritaka*. The latter form appears in one of my MSS.

[b] Rujjanaṁ] = rujanaṁ, from √*ruj*, "to pain."

[c] Pisetvâ].—Ger. of piseti, "to grind" (*Sk.* √pish).

[d] Tassa]—*i.e.*, of the stile.

[e] Jinâlaṅkâre].—The stanza quoted is not in the *Jinâlaṅkâra* itself, but in its Ṭikâ. Samatâyupekkhaṁ = samatâya + upekkhaṁ; nevicche = na + eva + icche. The translation of the stanza is:—"I pay honour to Buddha, gone to Nirvâṇa, abandoning birth and existence, whether organised or not organised, who desires not happiness or suffering or indifference (upekkha) through unconcern (samatâ, "sameness"), or that life which brings with it sensual gratifications, or that which brings no such gratifications." The *Jinâlaṅkâra* with its Ṭikâ was written by Buddharakkhita. A Ṭikâ by Buddhadatta is also mentioned.

[f] Catupaccayâ].—The four priestly requisites—*cîvara*, *piṇḍapâta*, *senâsana*, and *bhesajja*.

CHAPTER FIFTH.

[a] Osiñcati].—"To draw water," "to take water by dipping," the usual meaning being "to sprinkle."

[b] Aṅgatarâ].—Ablative, "beyond an aṅga (scriptural division)." The word may be treated also as a pl. fem. with the reading *bhâṇavaramattâ*.

[c] Saṅghadaṇḍako].—"A transgressor of priestly discipline," as he was taken for a merchant.

[d] Javanapañño].—"Quick-witted."

CHAPTER SIXTH.

[a] Upasseyyaphalake].—"On the plank or board serving as a support to the back." *Upasseyya* (properly *upassaya*) represents the *Sk*. upâśraya.

[b] Paṭiniyyâdeti].—"To make over to" (*Sk*. pratiniryâti).

[c] Sile patitthâya].—"What priest is there ripe in intelligence and energetic—a man of profound wisdom, established in the precepts and advancing his tranquillity and spiritual insight—who can unravel this knot of corruption?" Sapañño = paṭisandhipañño; cittaṁ = samâdhi; paññaṁ = vipassanâpaññaṁ; jaṭaṁ = kilesaṁ.

[d] Acchariyabhûto].—"In a state of wonder," "wonder-stricken."

[e] Vimhayamâno].—Part. of vimhayati (*Sk*. vismayate), "to be surprised."

[f] Abhinnapaṭisambhidaṁ].—"Proficient in the four *paṭisambhidâs*, which are not to be understood by every one." The reading *pabhinna*° will also answer. The *Paṭisambhidâmagga* enumerates seventy-three different kinds of knowledge, sixty-seven being *sâvakasâdhâraṇâni*, six *asâvakasâdhâraṇâni*. The four *paṭisambhidâs* belong to the former. They are—(1) Atthapaṭisambhidâ, or a differentiating knowledge of sense and purport; (2) dhammapaṭisambhidâ, or a differentiating knowledge of the sense and purport of the texts (Pali) of the scriptures; (3) niruttipaṭisambhidâ, or a differentiating knowledge of grammar, idiom,

and exegesis; and (4) paṭibhânapaṭisambhidâ, or a differentiating knowledge of worldly sciences. The sixty-seven kinds of knowledge are *sutamayañânaṁ, sîlamayañânaṁ*, &c.; the six *asâvakasâdhâraṇâni ñâṇâni* are—(1) *indriyaparopariyatti*, (2) *sattânaṁ âsayanusaya*, (3) *yamakapaṭihâriya*, (4) *mahâkaruṇâsamapatti*, (5) *sabbaññutâ*, and (6) *anâvaraṇa*. The four *paṭisambhidâs* precede these six. *Paṭisambhidâ* implies "differentiation by analysis for the purpose of precise elucidation." I notice in one MS. alternative explanations of *attha* and *dhamma*, the former being used with reference to "results," the latter with reference to "causes" and "first principles." *Vide* Hardy's *Manual of Buddhism*, p. 499.

[g] Sâsanantassa] = sâsanaṁ + tassa, the latter qualifying munino.

CHAPTER SEVENTH.

[a] Tâlâruḷhaka].—"A toddy-seller" (tâla + âruḷhaka).

[b] Kusalatikko].—"Expert," "versatile."

[c] Mahacetiyassa].—The one erected by Vattagâmani, B.C. 89, called the Sîlasobbhakaṇḍakacetiya. The burning of Mahinda's writings most probably symbolises the destruction of the Sinhalese MSS. by the Malabars.

[d] Sakkaṭa].—"Sanskrit."

[e] Abhâsi].—The stanzas referred to have come down in a very corrupt and hybrid form in Burmese MSS. B.F.L. has—"Brahivattasûhinivattaphâlayagâthâ, kalyânimapasiccatamramyataṁ paccatâmâruddhaprayamatapâsevattamappaddhakânâ, yovemyañjalîrentevatayassoḍḍhodaneyâsanaṁ, olokesiruecanayathâmatimâmoddhenapâlipata, ñasasiyañcagâravakkhatvâsappurisâsamâhithâmâ, raghasantocasukkhasantibuddhasissâvuttamâpamavamâti." P. has—"Brashyanidâḷunibrashyatthagâvâkunyânivasitañcatubrashyavacatvaṁ, seṭṭhashyamabyattakaṁyâcamyañjahvesavotirilokosîrasâniyaṁmahimaṁsuddhodhanassaputto bhagavati, saṅkhalikhitasadisaṁsâsanaṁmyattenasattahimâlimratta, attânaṁcandanasadisenasîlenaattânaṁsulimrattaathavâattânaṁmatovaratarohoti." The version in S.D.P. is as follows:—"Brashyanidâlunibrashyatthagâpâ kunyâsivâsitañcatubrashyâcatvaṁseṭṭhashyamaṁprattakaṁ, yâcamyañcalivesavotaṁparivesavotariloko, sirasâniyaṁmahimaṁsuḍḍhodhanassaputto, bhagavatisaṅkhalikkhitasadisaṁsâsanaṁmyattenasattahimâlamrittaattânaṁcandanasadisenasîlenaattânaṁsulamritta, athavâattânaṁsannirujjitvâmatovaratarohoti." These are literatim transliterations, which, in the absence of the Sinhalese text, makes the attempt of restoration to the original Sanskrit a task of some difficulty. Had the Burmese copyists been acquainted with the conventional system by which Sankrit can be precisely transliterated by means of Burmese characters, no such literary puzzle as we have now before us would have been presented for solution. From a *Nissaya*, I gather the meaning of the version in P. and S.D.P. to be:—"Subsisting as a porter, a cowherd, a water-drawer, or by serving

the learned is excellent. I beg you to let me hold up my hands in adoration. Let not the three worlds by means of the seven offences disgustingly besmear the conch-shell-like religion of the adorable one, the son of Suddhodhana,—a religion worthy always to be reverenced by the head. Besmear yourselves with virtue that is like sandal-wood; otherwise destroying yourselves, death is better." "Sattehi" is explained by "sattehi âpattikhandhehi." The following is a tentative restoration of the Sanskrit ślokas, the versification being *upajâti*:—

Preshyanidhâraṇena preshyarthagavâ
kuṁbhanivâsitañcaturasevakatvaṁ
śreshṭhasya mampratikâmiu
yâcamyañjalivesaṁ vaḥ
trilokaśîrshaniyammyamahimnaḥ
Śuddhodanasya putrabhagavatâ
śaṅkhalikhitasadṛiśaṁ śâsanaṁ
mṛidhrenenassaptabhirmâ limpatâ-
tmânañcandanasadṛiśena śilena
âtmânaṁ sulimpatâthavâtmânaṁ
śanirujjhitvâ mṛitirvarataro bhavati.

CHAPTER EIGHTH.

a Mayupanissâya] = mayaṁ + upanissâya.

b Niyamâgato].—My MSS. have niyâmagato also. One MS. has niyamo gato. The reading is very likely nirâmâkato, "bliss-producing" (*Sk.* nir + âma or âmaya). The letters *y* and *g* are often phonetic errors in Bur. MSS. for *r* and *k*. But *cf. Jinâlaṅkâra*, v. 5—

Visuddhakhandhasantâno
Buddho ti niyamo kato;
khandhasantânavisuddhîsu
guṇo ti niyamo kato.

c Siṅgâlâ] = sigâlâ, "jackal."

d Ânâpânaṁ].—"Exhalation and inhalation," not "inhalation and exhalation," as in Childers's Dictionary (*cf. vâtapânaṁ*, "a window"). The word is equal to "assâsapassâso." The *Paṭisambhidâmagga* defines it thus:—"Ânan ti assâso passâso no; pânan ti passâso assâso no." The reference is to the meditation known as the *soḷasavatthukaânâpânasatisamâdhi*. The following is from *Paṭisambhidâmagga*:—"Cittaṁ vikkhepaṁ na gacchati padhânañca paññâyati payogañca sâdheti visesaṁ adhigacchati, seyyathâ pi same bhûmibhâge rukkho nikkhitto hoti taṁ puriso kakacena chindeyya rukkhe phuṭṭhakakacadantânaṁ vasena purisassa sati upaṭṭhitâ hoti âgate vâ gate vâ kakacadante na manasi karoti, âgatâ vâ gatâ vâ kakacadantâ aviditâ na honti, padhânañca paññâyati payogañca sâdheti; same bhûmibhâge nikkhitto rukkho evaṁ tathâ upanibbhandanâ nimittaṁ daṭṭhabbaṁ. Kakacadantânaṁ pavatti yathâ evaṁ tathâ assâsapassâsâ daṭṭhabbâ." See treatment of this subject in the seventh section of *Visuddhimagga.*

° Dvipaduttamo].—"Having two excellent feet." This refers to the hundred and eight *lakkhaṇas* on the soles of Buddha's feet. A Bur. MS. gives them as follows :—

Satthi ca sirivaccho[1] ca nandiyâvattam eva ca
sovatthiko[2] vaṭaṁso ca vaddhamânañca pîṭhakaṁ
aṅkusañceva pâsâdo toraṇaṁ chattam eva ca
khaggo ca tâlavaṇṭañca morahatthakabîjanî
uṇhissaṁ maṇi pattañca dâmaṁ niluppalaṁ tathâ
rattasetuppalañceva padumaṁ puṇḍarikaṁ tathâ
puṇṇaghaṭo puṇṇapâti samuddo ca cakkavâḷaṁ
Himavâ ceva Sumeru suriyo candimâ tathâ
nakkhattâ caturo dîpâ dvisahassaparittakâ
cakkavati setasaṅkho macchânaṁ yugalaṁ tathâ
cakkaṁ sattamahâgaṅgâ mahâselâ mahâsarâ
supaṇṇako saṁsumâro[3] dhajo paṭâkameva ca
pâṭaṅkî[4] haribîjanî kelâsapabbato tathâ
sîharâjâ byaggharâjâ Valaho ca Uposatho
Bâsukinâgarâjâ ca haṅso ca usabho tathâ
Erâvaṇo makâro ca harinâvâ catumukhâ
savacchakâ tathâ gâvî kinnaro kinnarî pi ca
karaviko mayuro ca koñcarâjâ tatheva ca
cakkavâkadijo ceva jîvajîvanâmakâ ca
cha kâmâvacarâdevâ brahmalokâ ca soḷasa.

"A dagger-like sword, the magnificent mansion of Nirvâṇa, a rose-shaped flower with the marginal petals curving downwards and with left sweep, the symbol of three curved lines one over the other representing the arcs of the moon on the seventh, eighth, and ninth days of its waxing, a flower on stalks which grow upwards as well as downwards, a pinnacled platter, a stool or bedstead, an elephant goad, a turretted palace, a gate, an umbrella, a sword, a palm-fan, a hand-whisp of peacock's feathers, a coronal band or crown, a ruby, a bowl, a fringe, the blue water-lily, the red water-lily, the white water-lily, the *paduma* water-lily, the *puṇḍarika* water-lily, a full water-jar, a full dish, the ocean, a Buddhist world system, the Himalayas, Mount Meru, the sun, the moon, the constellations, the continent of trilateral-faced beings with lesser islands, the continent of circular-faced beings with lesser islands, the continent of crescent-faced beings with lesser islands, the continent of square-faced beings with lesser islands, Sakka as universal monarch, a white conch-shell, a pair of fishes, a cart-wheel, the seven[5] great rivers, the seven[5] great mountains,

---

[1] *Sk. śrivatsa.* [2] *Sk. svastika.*

[3] This is the usual form in Bur. MSS. = *Sk. śiśumâra.* The form *susumâro* ("child-slayer") is also met with. [4] *Sk. palyanka.*

[5] Each being taken separately as a sign.

the seven [1] great lakes, the Garuḷa bird, an alligator, a pair of pennants, a palanquin, a golden fan, the Kelâsa rock, the king of lions, the king of tigers, the horse Valaha, the elephant Uposatha, Vâsuki the dragon king, a goose, a bull, the elephant Erâvaṇa, the sea animal Makara, a golden boat, the four cardinal points, a cow with calf, a male Kinnara (having a bird's body with a human face), a female Kinnara, the sweet-voiced Karavika bird, a peacock, the crane king, a pelican (or ruddy goose), a swallow, the six [1] deva worlds, and the sixteen [1] Brahmalokas." Sometimes there are discrepancies in the enumeration. For the explanation of these discrepancies and notes on the signs, see the author's *The Burmese Buddhapâd*. In this connection *vide* Alabaster's *The Wheel of the Law*, p. 290; Hardy's *Manual of Buddhism*, p. 367; and Burnouf's *Lotus*, p. 625.

f Mârasenapamaddanâ].—Here the *ablative*. B.F.L. has pamaddito.

g Pamuñcaso].—"Released."

h Khaṇika].—"Momentary." The definition of death in *Vibhanga* is:—"Yâ tesaṁ tesaṁ sattânaṁ tamhâ tamhâ sattanikâyâ cuti cavanatâ bhedo antaradhânaṁ maccu maraṇaṁ kâlakiriyâ khandânaṁ bhedo kaḷevarassa nikkhepo jîvitindriyassa upacchedo idaṁ vuccati maraṇaṁ." Buddhaghosa in *Visuddhimagga* has:—"Ekabhavapariyâpannassa jîvitindriyassa upacchedo; yaṁ pana panetaṁ arahantânaṁ vaṭṭadukkhasamucchedasaṅkhâtaṁ samucchedamaraṇaṁ saṅkhâraṇaṁ khaṇabhaṅgasaṅkhâtaṁ khaṇikamaraṇaṁ; rukkho mato lohaṁ matan ti âdisu samuti maraṇaṁ."

i Vîthicittânaṁ].—Here *vîthi* (literally "road," "way") is used in a metaphysical sense, and signifies "thought production" (through the six *dvâras* [senses] in relation to the six *ârammaṇas*). See sec. 4 (Vîthisaṅgahavibhâga) in *Saṅkhepavaṇṇanâṭîkâ*.

---

[1] Each being taken separately as a sign.

THE END.

BUDDHAGHOSUPPATTI

OR

THE HISTORICAL ROMANCE

OF

THE RISE AND CAREER

OF

BUDDHAGHOSA

TRANSLATED BY

JAMES GRAY

PROFESSOR OF PALI, RANGOON COLLEGE
AND AUTHOR OF "THE NÎTI LITERATURE OF BURMA," ETC

LONDON:
LUZAC & CO.
PUBLISHERS TO THE INDIA OFFICE
1892

TRANSLATION.[1]

THE HISTORY OF BUDDHAGHOSA.

INTRODUCTION.

First paying honour to the Three Gems that dispel all evil, I shall write the authentic history of Buddhaghosa. Ye, good reverend sirs, assembled together, put aside other business, and, steadfast in faith, listen to that[2] history. He who hears the teaching of the good and acts up to it, receives distinction in the present existence and Nirvâṇa hereafter. Therefore should one attend respectfully to the account of Buddhaghosa, which sets forth the praise of the Omniscient One, and is conducive to the bliss of heaven and the bliss of emancipation.

CHAPTER FIRST.

BOYHOOD.

At first,[3] the reverend thera, Mahinda, having come to Ceylon with priests replete with supernatural powers, established Buddha's religion in this island of Ceylon in

[1] Since the text of *Buddhaghosuppatti* has been printed, I have had a MS. from Thatôn, which I have found very serviceable. Some of its readings are introduced in the foot-notes of this translation. The MS. is referred to as T.

[2] Instead of the reading *pahâya taṁ*, there occurs *pahâyadaṁ* = *pahâya* + *idaṁ*.

[3] *Sante* is understood with the introductory *evaṁ*, which refers to the sentiments of the introducting. *Evaṁ sante*, "this being so."

the 236th year after his Nirvâṇa. Having established it, and continuing to the end of his life, he fixed the faith in the hearts of many and underwent complete annihilation. After him the thera Buddhaghosa sprang up. How is his uprising to be known? It is said there existed once the village of Ghosa, not far from the Bodhi Tree. It had the name of Ghosa from its being the place of residence of a large number of cowherds' children. A certain king ruled in that village. His spiritual adviser was a Brahman, Kesi, who was an excellent teacher, lovable, and of pleasing deportment. His wife was known as Kesinî. In connection with these circumstances the ancients have said:—

> "The Brahman named Kesi, endeared to the king and a favourite of his, instructs him daily in the three Vedas; he had a Brahman wife, Kesinî by name, who was well accomplished; she was endeared to the Brahman, worthy of respect, and deserving of admiration."[1]

Whenever, on account of the religion of Buddha being recited in Sinhalese, others, not knowing that language, could not comprehend it, a certain thera, possessed of supernatural powers and completely devoid of taint, being aware of it, thought to himself, "Who is that great thera who will be able to turn the Word of Buddha into Mâgadhî on it being recited in Sinhalese?" And reflecting thus, he saw that the deva prince, Ghosa, living in the Tâvatiṁsa heaven, had the ability to put into Mâgadhî the Scriptures of Buddha, the Revered One, if repeated in Sinhalese. And even while he was reflecting, he presented himself before Sakka, the deva king.

[1] The reading *vananâlasâ* = *va* + *n* (euphonic) + *anâlasâ*, "assiduous," with the second *a* lengthened *metri causa*, is scarcely tenable in the light of my Thatôn MS. The reading *va anâsalâ* occurs in three MSS., and the meaning seems to be "not to be disgusted with;" hence "worthy of admiration." The etymology, however, seems doubtful. I am inclined to derive it from the root *nash*, "to destroy," and give it the meaning, "not harmful." *Anâsala* would, therefore, be equal to the Sk. *anâshaka*.

Sakka saluted him and asked, "Reverend sir, wherefore have you come?" He answered, "At present, O great king, the Word of the Revered One is difficult of comprehension, being recited in Sinhalese, but there is existing in the Tâvatiṁsa heaven a deva prince, Ghosa by name. He, having the wisdom of *Tihetupaṭisandhi*—that is, for re-birth in virtue of the absence of ignorance, hatred, and lust—and also the attributes of the past Buddhas, has the ability to put into Mâgadhî the Word of Buddha if recited in Sinhalese.

"Come then," said Sakka, and went into the presence of Ghosa, the deva prince, and, embracing[1] him, said, "A mahâthera propitiates you, and wishes you to go to the world of men."

The prince replied, "King of devas, I wish to go higher than the deva world; as residence in the world of men is full of suffering and worrysome, I, therefore, do not desire to go to their world, but I shall go if Buddha's Word is difficult of comprehension by others." In these words he gave his consent.

Having attained the prince's consent, Sakka announced it to the mahâthera, who thereupon went back.

This thera was at that time the Brahman Kesi's friend and family counsellor. At daybreak, taking with him his bowl and robe, he partook of food in the Brahman's house. On finishing, he said to the Brahman, "On the seventh day from this be not remiss; you will have a son who will be exceedingly meritorious and exceedingly wise." Having said this, he took his departure.

On the seventh day, being intent on it, Sakka died and obtained conception in the womb of Kesinî, the Brahman woman. He was born[2] after ten months. At the time of his birth the assembly of Brahmans, consisting of slaves, servants, and others, gave rise to pleasant exclama-

[1] *Aliṅgitvâ* is very likely the proper form. One MS. has *âliṅkitvâ*.

[2] The reading *gabbhato parinikkhami* is found in T. for *gabbhato nikkhami*.

tions, such as "eat," "drink," &c.; and so they gave him the name Ghosa.

Ghosa at the age of seven learnt the Vedas, and within seven years acquired proficiency in the three divisions. One day this young Brahman, Ghosa, was eating[1] peas seated in the spot sacred to Vishṇu. Other Brahmans, on seeing this, became very angry and exclaimed, "Eh! young Ghosa, wherefore are you seated eating peas in the place sacred to our teacher Vishṇu. If you do not know the measure of your own dignity, how will you know the three Vedas?"

Ghosa, seated as he was eating peas, uttered this stanza, questioning the Brahmans on a point having relation to Vishṇu:—

> "The pea itself is Vishṇu; what is it that is called Vishṇu? Of these two how can I know which is Vishṇu?"

Hearing this, the Brahmans kept looking at each other, and, being unable to reply, were silent. Thereupon some of the Brahmans told[2] Kesi about Ghosa. Kesi asked his son, "What, dear, did you act so?" "Yes, dear father," returned the son. Kesi conciliated the Brahmans, saying, "Look to me; be not angry; he knows[3] nothing," and then dismissed them.

One day, taking his son along with him, Kesi went to instruct the king in the Vedas. Ghosa went along with his father with a goat-skin for sitting on. While instructing the king, Kesi came across a knotty point in a certain place in one of the Vedas, and not comprehending its sense or purport, and being in doubt, took leave of the king and returned to his own house.

Ghosa, aware of his father not making out the knotty point, elucidated the difficulty by means of his own ability

[1] T. reads *bhuñji*.

[2] T. has *ârocayiṁsu*.

[3] *Jânâsi* should, no doubt, be *jânâti*, unless it be supposed that Kesi turns off from his speech to the Brahmans and addresses Ghosa.

and wrote[1] down the signification on a palm-leaf manuscript book. On seeing the writing, Kesi knew the sense and purport of the Vedic passage, and was glad. The knotty point became manifest in the Brahman's mind. He then asked his attendants, "By whom has this been written?"

The attendants replied, "Dear master, by whom except your son has the writing been executed?"

Kesi asked his son, "My dear, has this writing been executed by you?"

"Yes, dear father," says he.

The father, being extremely pleased, uttered two stanzas in praise of his son:—

> "Thou, though young, art renowned as wise; he whose son thou art, as being most exalted, is unrivalled among men.
>
> "Now art thou blessed, having established thyself as an immortal; thou art even my father; I am as thy son."

Having praised his son thus, he told the king about him. The king, on hearing the circumstance, was exceedingly glad, and, embracing Ghosa and pressing him to his breast, kissed him on his head and said, "Be thou[2] my son, dear; I am thy father." And then he uttered this stanza:—

> "Among Brahmans, thou, dear, art most excellent and exalted. I am delighted with thee on account of thy wisdom; I shall give thee a fine village."

Here ends the first chapter, containing an account of the boyhood of Buddhaghosa.

[1] For *potthake likhitvá ṭhapesi* T. has *potthake likhi*. It may be here remarked that the root *likh*, "to write," is treated in Bur. MSS., as if it belonged both to the *first* and the *third* class of verbs. Hence the base *likkha*.

[2] T. has *hohi*, not *hosi*.

CHAPTER SECOND.

ADMISSION TO THE PRIESTHOOD.

AFTER that, the young Brahman Ghosa, in learning the Vedas, got off six thousand pâdas daily. One day, the Mahâthera, the friend of the Brahman Kesi, came, according to custom, to the latter's house for his food and remained in the middle of it. A young Brahman carried off Ghosa's rug, and, pointing it out, presented it to the Mahâthera to sit on. The Mahâthera, though indifferent about it, sat on Ghosa's rug. Ghosa, noticing this, became mighty angry, just as if he were holding a snake by its tail and dashing it on the ground. Becoming thus angry and not able to restrain himself, he spoke abusively, "This bald-headed priest is shameless; he knows not how far to go! Why does my father feed him? does he know this tenet of mine, or does he know any other?" Having spoken thus derogatively of the Mahâthera, he thought as follows, "I shall ask him about the tenet when he has finished eating and removed[1] his hand from the bowl."

Then, when the Mahâthera had finished eating and removed his hand from the bowl, and was still seated, Ghosa asked him, "You, reverend bald-head, do you know the Vedic tenet, or do you know any other?"

The Mahâthera, on hearing these words, became exceedingly joyous and said, "Dear Ghosa, I know your Vedic tenet, and I also know another."

"If," said Ghosa, "you know the Vedic tenet, repeat it."

[1] The reading *nihaṭa* for *oṇita* occurs.

The Mahâthera then recited from the three Vedas, touched upon the beginning, middle, and end of them, and gave a clear exposition of the Vedic Scriptures as explained[1] by the wise, being like a ball of entangled thread. The recitation over, the Mahâthera washed his mouth with water from his water-pot and sat down.

Ghosa, seeing the thera, grew ashamed and said again, "I am desirous to know your tenet; rehearse it."

The Mahâthera, in order to satisfy him, rehearsed the *mâtikâ* of the *Abhidhammapiṭaka,* and after discriminating between the three *mâtikâs*—*i.e.*, of the *kusala*, *akusala*, and *abyâkata dhammas*—he said, "Dear Ghosa, what is called *kusala* is characterised by results that are blameless, conducive to the demolition of demerit, the means of purification, the producer of what is desirable, and leads to the attainment of a happy lot (*i.e.*, Nirvâṇa) ; what is *akusala* is characterised by undesirable and blameworthy results, is not the means of purification and the producer of mental enlightenment, but leads to the attainment of misery ; *abyâkata,* or what is indifferent, is characterised by being the reverse of the other two, being without consequences ; or by me is here set forth the fourfold[2] *kusala,* formulated by Muni, full of wisdom, controlled in his senses, and ever the inciter of what is meritorious :—

> "Whatever evil mental tendency has been declared by Buddha, who has parted with merit and demerit (by the attainment of Nirvâṇa) and excellently brought about good from evil—that is declared by me."
>
> "The Jina who has differentiated the attainment of actions into *kusala* and *akusala*, has set forth the mental tendency to the performance of actions accompanied by *kusala* and *akusala* and actions unaccompanied by *kusala* and *akusala*, and has, moreover,

---

[1] *Viniveḍo* is an adjective of the verb *vinivedati*, "to make known."

[2] *Catubhûmakaṁ* is used in reference to *kâma*, *rûpa*, *arûpa*, and *lokuttara*. In this relation *Dhammasaṅgaṇi* may be advantageously consulted.

> pointed out the mental tendency to the performance or non-performance of actions beneficial or unbeneficial differentiated from those that produce *kusala* and *akusala*—that too is set forth by me."

"Thus *kusala* is twenty-one fold, *akusala* twelve-fold, consequences (*vipâka*) thirty-six fold, and mental action (*kriyâ*) twenty-fold." In these words the Mahâthera pointed out the Excellent Law.

Ghosa, having listened to the *Abhidhammamâtikâ*, was perplexed and said, "What, reverend sir, is the name of this tenet of yours?"

"This, friend, is Buddha's tenet."

"Is Buddha's tenet," Ghosa asked, "to be acquired by a layman like myself?"

The other replied, "The tenet of Buddha can be learnt by a monk like myself, for holiness is wanting to a layman, and there are many obstacles."

One day Ghosa reflected on various passages of the three Vedas, considered the beginning and middle, but not the end, and, while reflecting, he exclaimed—

> "The creed of Buddha is invaluable; the creed of Buddha pleases me; by resorting to Buddha's creed, people are freed from all suffering!"

And when he had reflected thus, he saluted his parents and asked to be allowed to adopt the ascetic life. On receiving a rebuff, he made frequent requests, and afterwards said, "Dear parents, on becoming a monk, I shall learn Buddha's religion, and after I have got it off by heart I shall turn layman and return."

The parents then took him along with offerings, and leading him to the hermitage of the Mahâthera, made him over, saying, "This is thy grandchild;[1] he desires to become a monk; give him holy orders."

[1] *Nettâ*, for *nattâ* (Sk. *naptâ*), "grandson," is the form in all my MSS. I believe I have met the same form elsewhere.

The Mahâthera then removed his beard, and with moist sandal-wood powder removed from him the odour of laymanship, and making him wear a white robe, gave him the *Tacakammaṭṭhâna*[1]—"skin meditation"—for contemplation and admitted him to the priesthood.

"What, reverend sir," asked Ghosa, "is this *Tacakammaṭṭhâna?*"

The Mahâthera said, "It is the contemplation of the hair of the face and head, of the hair on the skin, of the nails, of the teeth, of the skin. Inasmuch as the *Tacakammaṭṭhâna* has not been abandoned by all the Buddhas—indeed, all the Buddhas, seated on the *seat of wisdom* (*bodhipallaṅke*), attained to the knowledge of the three *lakkhaṇas* through *Tacakammaṭṭhâna*, and came to the realisation of the *fruit of the first step in sanctification:* therefore has it been affirmed by the Revered One—

> "*Tacakammaṭṭhâna* has been taught by the Omniscient One; by having recourse to *Tacakammaṭṭhâna* one is freed from all suffering; therefore should one practise the most excellent *Tacakammaṭṭhâna*, full of essential worth;[2] by practising it he attains *Nirvâṇa*."

Ghosa, hearing this, went on practising *Tacakammaṭṭhâna*, and being established in the Three Refuges, steadfast in the ten precepts, and firm in faith, gave rise to the *three Lakkhaṇas* by means of the five *Kammaṭṭhânas*, and becoming firm in the religion of Buddha, he put faith in it and told the Mahâthera, "Reverend sir, the religion of Buddha puts an end to transmigration; it is the means of bringing about the destruction of suffering in all existences; this is known to me. My Vedas are without essential worth; they are void; they are without permanence; they have been relinquished by the Buddha and other saints."

[1] T. has *tacapañcakammaṭṭhâna*, a reading supported by the context lower down.

[2] T. gives *sâtasamataṁ* for *sâdhusammataṁ;* for *bhâvento* in the next line of the text, it has *bhavato*.

And so he became a monk; and thenceforth day by day got off sixty thousand pâdas, and in the space of a month completed the acquirement of the Three *Piṭakas.* Having done so, he, on coming of age, received ordination and obtained permanent[1] efficiency in the four *paṭisambhidas* or *differentiating analyses.* In all Jambudîpa he was known by the name Buddhaghosa. And he was lovable and estimable among gods and men; wherefore have the ancients said—

> "One Buddhaghosa by name, like Buddha in the world, was born of Brahman lineage near the Bodhi Tree; he was honoured by gods and men, honoured by Brahmans, honoured, too, by the priesthood; ever doth he obtain honour."

Here ends the second chapter, describing Buddhaghosa's admission into the Church and his having received ordination from his preceptor.

[1] Literally "not to be destroyed," "not to be impaired."

CHAPTER THIRD.

KESI'S CONVERSION.

ONE day the thought occurred to Buddhaghosa while he was alone and retired, "Is my or my preceptor's wisdom superior in regard to the Word of Buddha?" The preceptor, who was free from all sin, knew his thought then by his own internal perception, and remarked, "Now, Buddhaghosa, your thought does not please me; if you reflect on it, you will know that it is not becoming a priest; forthwith beg my pardon."

Hearing the words of his preceptor, Buddhaghosa became afraid and agitated, and addressed him respectfully, "This is my fault; pardon me, reverend sir."

The preceptor replied, "If you are to appease me, go to the island of Ceylon, translate the Word of Buddha from the language of Ceylon to that of Mâgadha, and then shall I be appeased." And ho romained silent.

Buddhaghosa said, "I would go to Ceylon if you wish it, but, reverend sir, until I convert my father from his heterodoxy, till then permit me to continue here." Having spoken so, he took leave of his preceptor and went home.

Kesi the Brahman, on seeing him, thought, "My son must now have become a layman; my son's face looks complacent," and being pleased, asked him, "Now will you leave the church and become[1] layman?"

When Buddhagosa heard this he remained silent. On going to his own residence, he had two brick compartments made, a brick roof constructed aloft, the walls plastered with mud, the building strengthened with

[1] *Bhavissati* is a wrong reading for *bhavissasi*.

planking,[1] and fixed two bolts inside and outside of one of the rooms. He placed fire, a pot, rice, water, milk, curd, butter, &c.; and after setting up a mechanical contrivance, he made his father enter the room, and closed the door by means of a string attached to the mechanism.

Kesi the Brahman asked, "My dear, I am your father; why do you act so?"

"True, you are my father," answered Buddhaghosa; "but as you are heterodox, not graciously disposed towards Buddha's Word, and unbelieving, I have therefore inflicted this punishment."

"I do not entertain a false belief," replied Kesi. "Open the door."

"I will open the door," said Buddhaghosa, "when, in case you are not heterodox, you have expressed the excellence of Buddha in the words, "*Iti pi so Bhagavâ,*" &c. And he frightened his father with the fear of hell, saying, "Dear father, you will fall into the Avîci hell on your death if you do not abandon your heresy." Moreover, reproaching his father again with heterodoxy, he gave utterance to these stanzas:—

> "When the crested sweet-voiced peacock is not seen, they then honour[2] the crow with offerings of flesh and fruit.
>
> "But when a peacock full of essential worth has come to Mount Meru, then the honour and worth of a crow are lost.
>
> "Until Buddha, the King of Law and Light-Giver, has not appeared, till then have some paid extensive honour to Samaṇas and Brâhmanas.

---

[1] *Badarena saṅkhâretvâ.* One is inclined to wonder if this is not intended as equivalent to the Sk. *pradraveṇa saṁskâretvâ,* "doing up with a liquid substance" (such as varnish).

[2] *Apûjeyyuṁ* of the Bur. MSS. here and in a subsequent stanza of the text is properly *apûjeyuṁ* (3rd pl. aor.).

"When Buddha, full of essential worth, has pointed out the Law, the honour and the worth of the heterodox have disappeared.

"Just as, like unto the heterodox, fireflies shine in the dark fortnight, displaying their splendour,[1] and their light vanishes when full of rays the sun comes up, thus the many unorthodox here, like unto the fireflies and resembling the dark fortnight, display their excellence in the world.

"When Buddha rises in the world, the unorthodox, hitherto of infinite radiance, lose their brightness, just as the firefly when the sun is up."[2]

Kesi, having suffered imprisonment for three days, brought to mind the excellence of Buddha as declared by his son, and having repeated the words *Iti*[3] *pi so*

[1] T. rightly reads, "dassayanti ca obhâsaṁ etesaṁ viya sobhanto." For *khajjopanakânaṁ*, it reads *khajjapansaṅghânaṁ*.

[2] The following is a metrical translation of the beautiful Pali verses:—

"A crow may shine an honour'd bird
On Meru's rocky mount;
But let the peacock show his plumes,
His worth then cannot count.

"Such offerings as flesh and fruit
Are only his by right;
The crested bird with sweet-toned voice
Provided is from sight.

"The King of Law and Sun of Truth
In glory is not seen
Where Samaṇas and Brahmaṇas
Their worth unduly ween.

"When Buddha comes replete with worth,
Lays down the Law of Truth,
Then heretics are put to shame,
Their honour lose forsooth.

As fireflies in a darksome night
Their brightness shed around,
But with the rising beams of day
No ray of light is found:

"So glory wanes for heretics,
Who like the fireflies are,
And Buddha's light is all the light
That shines both near and far."

[3] "*Iti pi so Bhagavâ.*" The full text is to be found in *Dhajaggasutta* of the *Parittaṁ*. It runs as follows: "Ahañca kho bhikkhave evaṁ vadâmi; sace tumhâkaṁ bhikkhave araññagatânaṁ vâ rukkhamûlagatânaṁ vâ suññâgâragatânaṁ vâ uppajjeyya bhayaṁ vâ chambhitattaṁ vâ lomahaṁso vâ mameva tasmiṁ samaye anussareyyâtha—'Iti pi so Bhagavâ arahaṁ sammâsambuddho vijjâcaraṇasampanno sugato lokavidû anuttaro purisadammasârathi satthâ devamanussânaṁ Buddho Bhagavâ ti.'" The translation is: "I tell you so, O priests, if on your going to the forest, the foot of a tree, or a solitary residence, there arise fear, consternation, or horripilation, at that time you should call me to mind as follows:—'He, indeed, the Revered One, is sanctified, omniscient, replete with knowledge and good practices; he is Sugata, the 'Well-conducted,'

Bhagavâ, &c., he became of blameless belief in the Three Refuges, said, "Henceforth I am going to a life-giving refuge," and addressed Buddhaghosa thus, "This Bhagavâ is my Teacher; I am his devotee." Through the excellence of Buddha he entertained a repugnance for his unorthodoxy and became established in the *fruition of the first path of saintship.*

Buddhaghosa opened the door, bathed his father with scented water, paid honour to him with scented flowers, &c., and thus wiped off his offence.

After his attainment to the state of Soâtpan, Kesi uttered these stanzas, glorifying the excellence of the Omniscient One:—

> "He who, having demolished all sin, is deserving of highest reverence, who is replete with the knowledge of all states and conditions—he, 'twice born,' is my Teacher.
>
> "He, the 'Well-conducted' (Sugata), who is replete with knowledge and good practices, and conversant with every state and condition in all the three worlds—he, 'twice born,' is my Teacher.
>
> "That Revered One who is more excellent than all, who is a subjugator of men as a horseman of horses—he, 'twice born,' is my Teacher."

Buddhaghosa, when he heard the words of his father, was pleased in mind, and congratulated him, exclaiming, "Well, well!"

Here ends the third chapter, describing the method adopted by Buddhaghosa for the emancipation of his father from heterodoxy.

world-wise, transcendental, the teacher and horseman-like subjugator of men, the venerated Buddha of gods and men.'"

CHAPTER FOURTH.

VOYAGE TO CEYLON.

HAVING established his father in the *fruition of the first path to saintship* and wiped off his offence, Buddhaghosa took leave of him and returned to his preceptor, by whom having been deputed to Ceylon, he continued as long as it suited him, and taking leave for the purpose of his journey to the island, he went to the port along with some merchants, embarked, and set out. On the very day of his departure, the Mahâthera Buddhadatta left the island of Ceylon. Thinking to himself that he must go[1] to Jambudîpa, he embarked with some merchants and was on his way back.

Buddhaghosa had traversed the great ocean in his vessel for three days. Buddhadatta, too, had been on the great ocean three days in his vessel on his return voyage. Through the supernatural power of Sakka and other devas, the vessels of the two theras, coming into collision, stood still.

The merchants then, observing this, stared at one another terror-stricken. Of the two theras, Buddhaghosa, coming out, noticed the terrified state of his friends the merchants, and inquired of the other merchants, "What monk, sirs, has come in your vessel?"

The merchants, the friends of Buddhadatta, said, "It is Buddhadatta."

[1] The quotation "Puna Jambudîpam agamâ" is evidently faulty. None of the MSS. has the right reading, which I take to be "Puna Jambudîpam âgamâmi," or more probably "Puna Jambudîpam âgamâmâ," the verb being in the first person plural. The copyist may have omitted the last *mâ* as a superfluity. "Âgamâmâ" is therefore restored.

Hearing this, Buddhadatta came out, and seeing the thera Buddhaghosa, became highly delighted and asked, "What, sir, is your name?"

Buddhaghosa replied, "I am Buddhaghosa."

"Whither are you bound?"

"I, dear sir, am bound for Ceylon."

"Wherefore are you going?"

"I am going to translate the Scriptures of Buddha which are in the Sinhalese language into the language of Mâgadha."

"I," said Buddhadatta, "was deputed to go and translate the Scriptures of Buddha from Sinhalese and to transcribe them in the Mâgadhî language, but I have obtained only the works *Jinâlaṅkâra*, *Dantavaṁsa*, *Dhâtuvaṁsa*, and *Bodhivaṁsa*, not the *Aṭṭhakathâs* and *Ṭîkâs*. If, sir, you are to render the Sinhalese version of Buddha's religion into the language of Mâgadha, render into the latter the *Aṭṭhakathâs* and *Ṭîkâs* of the Three *Piṭakas*." He encouraged Buddhaghosa thus, and made over to him the myrobolan, the iron style, and the stone which had been given to himself by Sakka, the king of the devas. He moreover said, "If ever you have an eye affection or an aching of the back, rub the myrobolan on the stone and apply it on the part that pains, and your affection[1] will disappear," and, pointing out to him the miraculous efficacy of the style, he gave it to him.

Buddhaghosa then heard the following introductory stanza of the *Jinâlaṅkâra* in adoration of Buddha:—

> "I pay honour to Buddha, gone to Nirvâṇa, abandoning birth and existence, what is organised or not organised, who desireth not happiness, or suffering, or indifference through unconcern, nor that life accompanied by sensual gratifications, or the life in which such gratifications are wanting."

Having heard this, he said, "Reverend sir, your treatise

[1] T. has *tuyhaṁ kâye uppanno rogo*.

is written very stylishly; people of respectability will be unable afterwards to know its meaning; by the ignorant it will be most difficult of comprehension."

"Reverend Buddhaghosa," said Buddhadatta, "prior to yourself I went to Ceylon to work up the religion of Buddha; I am of short life; I shall not live long; I shall, therefore, not be able to carry it out; do you execute it thoroughly."

On the conclusion of the conversation between the two theras with regard to the Word of Buddha, the two vessels belonging to the merchants moved away of themselves. Of the two, Buddhaghosa's went in the direction of Ceylon; that of Buddhadatta made for Jambudîpa. The latter arrived there with the merchants. He lived[1] only a few days, fulfilled priestly duties, and, on his death, was born in the Tusîta city. The merchants, in virtue of their having provided the four priestly requisites for the thera, were born, on their death, in Tâvatiṁsa abode.

Buddhaghosa with the merchants he accompanied arrived at the island of Ceylon, moored his vessel in the vicinity of Dvijaṭhâna and remained there.

Here ends the fourth chapter, relating
the arrival of Buddhaghosa
in Ceylon.

[1] T. reads *vasanto yeva* for *vasitvâ*.

CHAPTER FIFTH.

BUDDHAGHOSA AS A WITNESS.

WHILE Buddhaghosa was staying there (at Dvijaṭhâna) for a few days, two slave-women, belonging to Brahmans in Ceylon, took their pots and went to fill water. One of the two, having first filled water at the ford, was coming up. As she was coming up, the other slave-woman was going down to the ford in hot haste. The jar of the one who was ascending, being struck by hers, broke. The woman whose jar was broken became enraged with her and spoke discourteously, saying, "You are the child[1] of a slave, you are the child of a harlot, you are as ignorant as a cow!" She went on speaking so, making use of a large number of abusive epithets.

The other, hearing herself reviled, became incensed and spoke in the same abusive, opprobrious fashion. In a short time the language of abuse and opprobrium employed[2] by the two slave-women exceeded an *aṅga*, being of the length of a *bhâṇavâra*.

Buddhaghosa, hearing this bandying of abuses, thought, "There is no one else here but I; these slave-women abusing each other will make me a witness and tell their husbands; they will then question me; when asked, I shall show their abuses in writing." Thereupon he wrote down the abusive speech of the two in the manuscript

[1] *Dâsiputtosi* is the reading of all the MSS.; for *gaṇikâya puttosi* T. reads *gaṇikaputti*.

[2] *Kathitvâ* should be *kathitâ*.

note-book[1]—"One of the two made use of such an abuse; the other such an abuse. . . ."

By abusing each other for a considerable time, they grew weary, went home, and told their husbands.

The husband of the slave-woman whose jar was broken, being dissatisfied, quarrelled with the husband of the other, and, going to the king's tribunal, reported the matter to him.

The king, being unable to settle the case, asked, "Who is your witness?"

One of the two women said, "A foreigner, one who has transgressed priestly discipline, is at the landing-place—he is my witness."

The other also referred to the same thera, and made a similar intimation to the king.

The king then sent an emissary to have the thera questioned.

Buddhaghosa, without saying, "The abusive language used by these two Brahman women has been accurately heard by me, but we monks do not take notice of things," made over into the hands of the emissary his manuscript note-book containing his written statement of abuses and said, "Friend, show this note-book to the king."

The messenger took it and showed it to the king, who, on hearing it read, questioned the two slave-women—"Eh, women! has abuse like this been truly uttered by you?"

"It is true, your honour," they responded.

The king said, "The one carrying the heavy weight should have been kept at a distance by the one carrying the light weight." On making the declaration he inflicted punishment on the Brahman slave-woman whose jar was not broken.

Being desirous to see the thera, the king asked the

[1] *Lañjanapotthakaṁ*, a note-book. *Lañjana* appears as a permanent form in Burmese MSS. for the Sk. *lâñchana*. I notice the same form in a Talaing work.

Brahmans, "Where does he who has shown himself so quick-witted reside?"

The Brahmans, being unorthodox, were envious of the thera's excellence and said, "This offender against priestly discipline, your majesty, has come with the object of trading; it is not advisable for you to see him."

The king, on hearing this, was satisfied with the thera's excellence, and uttered two stanzas in praise of him—

> "Among the many priests of Ceylon, no priest like him has ever before been seen here.
>
> "He attains heaven who gives offerings to and reveres one so virtuous, clever, and most self-denying."

The king remained silent after having thus expressed in two stanzas the excellence of Buddhaghosa.

Here ends the fifth chapter, describing the testimony given by Buddhaghosa, through his wisdom, in relation to the two Brahman slaves.

CHAPTER SIXTH.

PERMISSION TO TRANSLATE THE SCRIPTURES.

AFTER that the thera Buddhaghosa went to the archbishop of Ceylon to pay his respects. Having done so, he sat on one side behind the priests who were engaged in listening to the *Abhidhamma* and *Vinaya Piṭakas* from the archbishop.

One day the archbishop, while giving instruction to the priests, came across a knotty point in the *Abhidhamma*. Not seeing nor comprehending the meaning of it, he was perplexed, and dismissing the priests, went into his cloister and sat down reflecting on the difficult point.

Just when he went in, Buddhaghosa, aware that the Mahâthera did not comprehend the knotty point, got up from his seat, wrote down the drift and signification of it on the board for resting the back against, and went away to his vessel.

The archbishop again and again considered the meaning of the knotty point, but discovered neither the signification nor the purport. Just, however, on his coming out from his cloister, the writing on the board caught his eyes. On seeing it he asked the monks, "By whom has this been written?"

"It must be by the foreign priest, reverend sir," replied the monks.

"Where has he gone?" asked the archbishop, and then commanded the monks, "Look for him; bring him and present him to me."

The monks, searching for him, saw him, and giving him encouragement, brought him before the archbishop.

The archbishop asked, "Is it true what is said, that this writing is by you?" And when Buddhaghosa replied, "Yes, reverend sir," he added, "Then the assembly of priests has to learn[1] the three *Piṭakas* from you," and made him over to the priesthood.[2]

Buddhaghosa refused him, saying, "I, reverend sir, have not come to Ceylon from Jambudîpa for instructing in the priesthood,[3] but I have come to translate the religion of Buddha from the language of Ceylon and transcribe it in the Mâgadha tongue." In these words he announced to him the reason of his coming.

Hearing this, the archbishop was exceedingly pleased, and replied, "If you have come saying you will transcribe the religion in the Mâgadha tongue, make a compendium of the three *Piṭakas* from the following stanza uttered by Buddha, the Revered One, and show it to me:"—

> "What priest is there ripe in intelligence and energetic, a man of profound wisdom, established in the precepts, and advancing his tranquillity and spiritual insight, who can unravel this knot of corruption?"

Buddhaghosa answered, "Very well," and went to his dwelling-place.

On that day, on account of a favourable asterism during the waxing moon,[4] Buddhaghosa commenced with the text, "*Sîle patiṭṭhâya,*" &c. ("*What priest is there,*" &c.), and easily wrote the treatise *Visuddhimagga.* Having finished it, he said to himself, "I shall lay it aside," and went off to sleep.

[1] In *sikkhitabbo* and in *sikkhanatthâya*, a little lower down in the text, we meet the Vedic usage of the root *siksh*, "to teach" instead of "to learn."

[2] T. has *bhikkhusaṅghaṁ tassa paṭiniyyâdeti*, which is a more reasonable reading.

[3] T. has *bhikkhusaṅghaṁ.*

[4] *Vattamânaccharâya* I took at first to be "in the present moment," "at once," but there is an astrological reference, and the reading must be *vaḍḍhamânacchâyâya*, "during the waxing moon," literally "in the increasing radiance."

Sakka, king of the devas, pilfered the *Visuddhimagga* which had been written and put away. The thera, on awakening and not seeing his treatise, very quickly wrote another edition by lamplight.[1] On finishing it, he placed it at his head and fell asleep. Sakka went stealthily off with it. Having slept a little, the thera again arose, but did not see it. It is said that, on the second watch of night setting in, Sakka, king of the devas, stole away the second treatise on the second occasion.

On arising and not seeing it, the thera in hot haste again wrote another edition of the *Visuddhimagga* by lamplight. After finishing it he tied it in his robe and slept. Sakka then deposited the two works he had previously taken away at the head of the thera and departed. Getting up at dawn and seeing the two editions written by him placed at his head, Buddhaghosa became pleased, and, after attending to his bodily ablutions, &c., took the two books, and, together with the one he had tied up in his robe, showed them to the archbishop of Ceylon.

It is said that in each[2] of the three books there are one million nine hundred and twenty-three thousand letters.

The archbishop, seeing the three, was surprised and asked, "Why are there three books?" On Buddhaghosa telling him the reason, he, being struck with amazement, had the three editions read out. In every place in the three where words were written by Buddhaghosa containing particles or prefixes, they were written down exactly the same, "a," "vi," &c., appearing alike. Seeing

[1] *Divâlokena* was a clerical error of the MSS. for *dîpâlokena*, "by lamplight." This is in keeping with the context, and T. supports the reading. The same remark applies to the word in the following paragraph of the text: "By daylight," therefore, is a wrong interpretation.

[2] A gloss reads *Tîsu ganthesu ekekaganthe kira*, &c. *Dasasahassâni* should be *dasasatasahassâni*, and says the letters of the *Visuddhimagga* are incalculable, but the wise have set them down at 1,923,000.

them so, the archbishop, being exceedingly pleased, gave permission to Buddhaghosa, saying, "Put the religion of Buddha, the Revered One, into the language of Mâgadha." And having given permission, he uttered two stanzas in praise of the excellence of his wisdom :—

> "He who sees such wisdom, capable of highest analysis and differentiation, and proficient in all states and conditions, he sees one like Buddha himself.
>
> "Mayest thou, replete with knowledge, being our superior, ever take in hand the religion of Buddha the Sage."

After that the thera was known to the people of the island by the name of "Buddhaghosa" ("the Voice of Buddha"). The ancients have therefore said—

> "By the name Buddhaghosa he was well known in the whole island; always the most exalted of men, like Buddha on the face of the earth."

Here ends the sixth chapter, giving an account of the permission granted to Buddhaghosa by the resident high priest of Ceylon to copy the Scriptures.

CHAPTER SEVENTH.

BUDDHAGHOSA'S OBJECT ATTAINED—HIS KNOWLEDGE OF SANSKRIT.

AFTER staying for a while in Ceylon, Buddhaghosa asked the assembly of priests for a suitable place for himself in order to write the Scriptures of Buddha the Sage. The Mahâthera gave him an iron structure to live in. It is said that the building had seven floors. Six of these floors were occupied by Mahâtheras. In what way six? One perfect in the precepts of purity lived in the second floor; one efficient in the *Dhutaṅgas* (the thirteen ascetic practices) in the third; one efficient in the *Suttapiṭaka* in the fourth; one efficient in the *Abhidhamma* in the fifth; one efficient in the *Vinaya* in the sixth; one efficient in *Jhâna* and devoted to the three[1] *Bhâvanâs* leading to the *fruitions of the four paths* resided in the seventh story. The ground-floor of the building was empty and unoccupied by any priest.

Buddhaghosa dwelt on its solitary under floor. It is said he was efficient in the *Dhutaṅgas* and in the whole of the Scriptures. And while residing there, he day by day wrote in Mâgadhî the religion of Buddha, the Revered One, translated from the language of the island.

Afterwards, while going early one day on his begging rounds, he saw some palm-leaves which had fallen off themselves,[2] and taking them, departed from the village in which he had gone about. It must be known that this was his practice.

[1] *Tilakkhaṇabhâvanâ* refers to the *kâya*, *citta*, and *paññâ bhâvanâs*.

[2] T. *vâ chaḍḍitatâlapaṇṇaṁ vâ*, or "palm-leaves thrown away."

One day a toddy-seller, learned, wise, and meritorious, noticing his procedure, scattered a number of palm-leaves, holeless and unbroken, in the place where he used to get his food in his bowl and concealed himself. The thera, after receiving food in his bowl, carried them off.

The toddy-seller followed him, saw the writing work on which he was engaged, and being pleased, took a basket of rice one day[1] and offered it to the thera, who addressed him as follows: "O devotee, the one who is stationed in the floor above mine is my superior; give the food to him."

Being thus commanded by the thera, he took the rice basket and gave it to the Mahâthera who remained on the upper floor.

In this manner the one basket of rice reached the reverend monk who resided on the seventh floor.

The monk residing on the seventh floor said to the toddy-seller, "Buddhaghosa on the lowest floor is of greater excellence than us; day by day he writes[2] the Scriptures of Buddha; give it to him."

On hearing this, the toddy-seller took the basket of rice, came down from the seventh story, and presented it again to Buddhaghosa.

"Well, well!" responded Buddhaghosa, and then divided the rice into six shares and made the toddy-seller give them to the six theras. This was his practice.

Buddhaghosa concluded the writing of the Scriptures in three months. After keeping Lent and celebrating *pâvaraṇâ*, he made them over to the archbishop.

The archbishop said, "Good! good!" in commendation of Buddhaghosa and recited two stanzas setting forth his excellence—

> "The religion, the word of the most excellent Buddha, is difficult of acquirement; by virtue of your translation we discern it easily.

---

[1] T. has *ekadivasamhi.*

[2] *Likhi ; tasseva* should be *likhantasseva.*

"Even as a blind man sees not equalities and inequalities on the ground, so we see not the religion as declared by Buddha."

Buddhaghosa, after that, had the works written by the thera Mahinda put into a heap in a sacred place near the Great Pagoda and set on fire. It is said that all the books written by the thera in the Sinhalese language were equal in height to seven elephants of middle size. The ancients say so, and it has been heard[1] by us as their declaration.

After setting fire to all the works compiled in Sinhalese, Buddhaghosa took leave of the assembly of priests with the object of seeing his parents, and saying, "I, reverend sirs, wish to go to Jambudîpa," prepared to embark along with the merchants.

Just when he was on the point of doing so, some resident priests of Ceylon spoke disparagingly of his proficiency in Sanskrit, remarking, "This thera, we imagine, knows only the religion of Buddha comprised in the Three *Piṭakas;* he knows no Sanskrit."

Hearing this disparaging conversation of theirs, Buddhaghosa's friends, the merchants, told him of it.

The thera, when he heard this, said, "Very well, very well!" and informed the resident archbishop of Ceylon, saying, "To-morrow, reverend sir, the Sabbath-day of the full moon, I shall discourse in Sanskrit; let the fourfold assembly be congregated in the yard of the Great Shrine."[2]

[1] The reading in T. is *sutabhûtaṁ* for *sutaṁ*.

[2] T. reads "catuparisâ mahâcetiyassa samîpe sannipatitâ hotu." By a reference in T. it appears that by *mahâceti* the great shrine erected B.C. 157, by Duṭṭhagâmaṇi, is intended. For an account of its construction *vide Mahâvaṁsa*, chapters xxviii. to xxx. The *Lohapâsâda*, in which Buddhaghosa is represented as having written the Scriptures, was the one erected by Saddhâtissa, the brother of Duṭṭhagâmaṇi. *Mahâvaṁsa*, chap. xxxiii. says :—

"Dîpe na lohapâsâdo sodhayïttha susaṅkhato;
Kâresi lohapâsâdaṁ so satthabhûmakaṁ puna;
Navutisatasahassaggho pâsâdo âsi so tadâ."

"The Lohapâsâda (of Duṭṭhagâmaṇi) did not hold together in good

Early in the morning, he ascended the pulpit for the purpose of displaying his knowledge of Sanskrit in the midst of the assembly, and standing therein gave forth these stanzas in Sanskrit:[1]—

> "Subsisting as a porter, a cowherd, a water-drawer, or by serving the learned is excellent. I beg you to let me hold up my hands in adoration; let not the three worlds by the seven offences[2] disgustingly besmear the conchshell-like religion of the adorable one, the son of Suddhodana—a religion worthy to be reverenced by the head; besmear yourselves with virtue that is like sandal-wood; otherwise destroying yourselves, death is preferable."

It is said that the quadruple extraordinary[3] wonders occurred in the case of Buddhaghosa. Which four?

(1.) If the assemblies of priests came for the purpose of seeing Buddhaghosa, they were gladdened by sight of him; (2.) if he discoursed among them on religion, they were delighted with what he said; (3.) when he remained silent, the assembly of priests were discontented; (4.) if the assembly of nuns, of male devotees, and of female devotees came to see Buddhaghosa, they were delighted by seeing him; and if he discoursed on the law among them, they were also delighted with what he said; but they were dissatisfied if Buddhaghosa remained silent: these are the four extraordinary, unexpected incidents

order; he (Saddhâtissa) rebuilt it as a seven-storied structure; the structure was then worth nine millions."

[1] T. says "Sakkaṭaganthêna missitvâ imâ gâthâyo abhâsi," he uttered these stanzas mixed with Sanskrit. We can scarcely take this assurance seriously, but do not wonder that it was made, considering the heterogeneous conglomeration of Sanskrit and Pali words in the corrupt text of the Burmese manuscripts.

[2] The seven kinds of offences are: — *Pârâjika*, *saṅghâdisita*, *pâcita*, *thûlaccaya*, *dukkaṭa*, *dubbhâsita*, and *pâṭidesani*. Buddhaghosa, no doubt, spoke in particular reference to *dubbhâsita* offences.

[3] The reading *abhûtadhamma*, "what is not to be," "what is impossible," hence "extraordinary," occurs in T. and elsewhere.

which occurred in Buddhaghosa's case, just as it happened in that of Ânanda. And therefore, even while he was discoursing, the four assemblies removed their raiments, pearl necklaces, and bangles,[1] and spread them at the feet of the thera by way of offering. The raiments, &c., given as offerings were in height, it is said, equal to seven elephants of medium size.

Buddhaghosa, having no desire for them, descended from the pulpit, saluted the assembly, took leave of the aged senior priest, and, embarking with the merchants, was bound for Jambudîpa. On his departure, people, beggars, mendicants, rahans, Puṇṇas, and others, took at pleasure the things that had been offered to the thera and went away

Here ends chapter seventh, describing the religious discourse by which Buddhaghosa displayed his knowledge of Sanskrit.

[1] "Veḷuriya" of *vatthaceḷamuttahâraveḷuriyâdîni*, is rightly given by T. as *valaya*, "a bangle," and the whole expression as *vatthâdîni muttahâravalayâdîni*.

CHAPTER EIGHTH.

RETURN TO INDIA.

HAVING displayed his knowledge of Sanskrit, Buddhaghosa was bound for Jambudîpa, and while proceeding in mid-ocean, he recited two stanzas for the purpose of conveying[1] instruction to the merchants:—

> "Just as we, depending on the vessel, traverse the ocean, and the vessel, depending on us, will reach harbour; so, depending on wisdom and on good deeds, which convey us comfortably to bliss, we are set down[2] on the shore of heaven."

On reaching port, Buddhaghosa took leave of his friends the merchants, and, with his bowl and robes, went into the presence of his preceptor. He apprised him of the transcript he had made of Buddha's religion, known as "Pariyatti." Thereupon, having absolved himself from the penalty imposed by the preceptor and wiped off his offence, he saluted him, and, taking leave of him, proceeded to his parents.

The parents, on seeing their son, saluted him, entertained him with luxurious food, forgave him his offence,

[1] T. gives *anusâsento* for *anusâsanto*.

[2] T. gives *patiṭṭhâma* for *patiṭṭhâya*, and it is a good reading. The two stanzas may be freely translated as follows:—

> "Men take to ships for distant lands
> The briny sea to cross;
> If sailors none, no port they find,
> But on the billows toss.
>
> "If to Nirvâṇa's blissful shore
> Our way we wish to take,
> By Wisdom's ship with Virtues mann'd,
> The voyage safe we make."

and, when they knew that they were to die, they, on the approach of death, called to mind the excellence of Buddha, were born in the Tusîta city, and dwell in a golden mansion. Some of the Brahmans, their attendants and slaves, being established in the admonitions of the thera Buddhaghosa, died and were born in the Devaloka; some passed away according to their deeds.

The thera, for the purpose of expressing his reverence for the Three Gems and displaying his delight in the good men in them, and, as if it was being declared "reverence to such an extent must be shown for the Three Gems," he, with a view to set forth their true nature, said—

> "The Revered One of pure lineage, he indeed is called Buddha; the Law, leading to bliss, preached by the Revered One, is the ninefold transcendental law."

As to the *Piṭakas* there are three—the *Vinaya*, the *Sutta*, and the *Abhidhamma;* of the *Nikâyas* five—the *Dîgha*, the *Majjhima*, the *Saṁyutta*, the *Aṅguttara*, and the *Khuddaka;* of *Aṅgas* nine—*Sutta*, *Geyya*, *Gâthâ*, *Veyyâkarana*, *Udâna*, *Ittivuttaka*, *Jâtaka*, *Abbhûta-dhamma*, and *Vedalla;* of *Dhammakhandas* eighty-four thousand; in the *Abhidhamma* forty-two thousand; in the *Vinaya* twenty-one thousand;[1] in the *Suttanta* twenty-one thousand. There are four assemblies; also four bodies established in the *Paths* and four established in the *Fruitions*, making up the sum of eight *Ariyas.*

Having thus indicated the true nature of the Three Gems, he uttered this stanza, testifying to his reverence for them:—

> "By holding up my hand even once in adoration of Buddha, his Law, and the priesthood, I am able completely to extinguish the fire of the pains of existence."

At the close of his words of reverence for the Three

[1] *Dvâdasasahassâni* should be *dve dasasahassâni.* *Vide* Hardy's *Eastern Monachism*, pp. 166–172, on the names and divisions of the *Tripiṭaka.*

Gems he uttered these following stanzas, setting forth the deeds of those practising deceit to maintain existence —those who in religious discipline are remiss—who are wicked and perform acts tending to the disparagement of the religion of the Revered One:—

> "As indeed base-born foxes eat not the flesh of the lion, king and chief of beasts, but worms produced in his body, being desirous to eat his flesh, eat it—not other beasts; so not heretics, though possessed of supernatural power, disparage the excellent Law of the Lion of the Sakyas, who attained to Nirvâṇa in the Buddhistic faith; but verily these wicked priests, smooth-shaven and wearing their patched-up apparel, it is they who disparage the excellent law pointed out by the Omniscient One." [1]

After thus showing the procedure of evil priests, performing acts for the disparagement of the religion of the Revered One, Buddhaghosa, for the object of pointing out to all creatures the practice of respiration and inspiration night and day, uttered this stanza—

> "By day a hundred thousand and eight hundred respirations and inspirations, and during the night the same number take place."

After pointing out this, he, being seated on his death-bed considering how long life [2] would hold out in him,

[1] The following is a metrical version:—

> "Not base-born foxes eat the flesh
> Of lion great and strong;
> Such feast is for the creeping worms
> That to his skin belong.
>
> "Not heretics with wondrous powers
> The Word of him revile—
> The Lion of the Sakya race,
> To Nirvâṇa gone the while.
>
> "But shaven priests with patched-up robes,
> Who in the fold exist,
> From evil speech against his Word
> Cannot, alas! resist."

[2] T. reads *nisinno attano âyusaṅkhâraṁ vicârento.*

ascertained it would be brief, and paying his respects to his preceptor and taking leave of him, he proceeded to the great Bodhi Tree, performed all ceremonial worship at its foot, and recited two stanzas in praise of it:—

> "Buddha, the Enlightened One, possessed of two excellent feet, attained to perfect knowledge, crushing the army of Mâra, by dependence on the Bodhi Tree.
>
> "He who shows respect to the Bodhi Tree and in worship is greatly reverential,[1] he, as it were, worships Buddha himself and is free from all suffering."

He praised the tree thus, and knowing the exact time of his death, he said to himself, "Death is of three kinds, *samuccheda*, *khaṇika*, and *sammuti*; of these, *samuccheda* is the death of one without taint; *khaṇika* is the momentary cessation of thought productions; *sammuti* is the ordinary death of all sentient beings; and," continued he, "of these, I am to die the common death."

Having thought so, he, on the day of his death, bringing to mind the precepts for him to observe, together with the excellence of Buddha, expired, was reborn in the Tusîta city, and now dwells in a golden mansion, twelve leagues in extent, attended by a thousand celestial nymphs.

When Metteyya as Bodhisat will here, in this world, attain perfect enlightenment, Buddhaghosa will become his disciple, the chief and most exalted, by virtue of his knowledge, surmounting all impediments in the laws of Metteyya, the Revered One (Bhagavâ). Seven times will he be set up by him in this place of pre-eminence as head disciple, Metteyya saying, "Of all my disciples, of all efficient in the *Vinaya*, of all of comprehensive knowledge, of all in whom knowledge is consummated, of those proficient in knowledge, Buddhaghosa is chief."

When the thera Buddhaghosa died, in order to burn his corpse, Rahans, Puṇṇas, all the gods and men, made a funeral pile with sandal-wood, and, putting upon it the

[1] T. has *atipûjayi* for *abhipûjayi* and *pamuñcato* for *pamuñcaso*.

bejewelled oblations,[1] placed the corpse together with its golden couch on the sandal-wood pile, and set fire to it with due respect. When his body had been cremated, men, Brahmans, and others took relics, and burying them in holy spots in the vicinity of the great Bodhi Tree, erected pagodas over them. All the people took delight in the excellence of the thera, and on their death, through virtue of their veneration of him, were reborn in Deva worlds, and, according to their deeds, are in the enjoyment of celestial glories.

After the time of the thera dwelling in the Tusîta city, former teachers, on account of ignorant people praising themselves and imagining themselves wise, saying, "We are wise," have given expression to three stanzas in reprehension of them—

> "On the death of Buddhaghosa, many, ignorant and foolish, over and over imagine '*We are wise.*'
>
> "But while Buddhagosa lived, even the wise possess not the radiance of wisdom, just as the moon in the jaws of Râhu.
>
> "Therefore, should a wise man abandon the praise of self, saying, '*I am wise;*' holding himself under control, he loses not happiness."

Here ends the eighth chapter, giving an account of the thera Buddhaghosa, replete in wisdom, penetration, quick-wit and humour, edited by the thera Mahâmangala, by his own wisdom, from the writings of ancient teachers.

[1] T. reads *aggiyâni* in the signification of "things used as fuel,' 'faggots."